Habits of Mind

Melinda Fine

Habits of Mind

Struggling Over Values in America's Classrooms

Jossey-Bass Publishers • San Francisco

Copyright © 1995 by Jossey-Bass Inc., Publishers, 350 Sansome Street,
San Francisco, California 94104. Copyright under International, Pan
American, and Universal Copyright Conventions. All rights reserved.
No part of this book may be reproduced in any form—except for brief
quotation (not to exceed 1,000 words) in a review or professional
work—without permission in writing from the publishers.

> Substantial discounts on bulk quantities of Jossey-Bass books
> are available to corporations, professional associations, and other
> organizations. For details and discount information, contact the
> special sales department at Jossey-Bass Inc., Publishers.
> (415) 433–1740; Fax (415) 433–0499.

For sales outside the United States, please contact your local
Paramount Publishing International office.

Manufactured in the United States of America on Lyons Falls
Pathfinder Tradebook. This paper is acid-free and 100 percent
totally chlorine-free.

Library of Congress Cataloging-in-Publication Data

Fine, Melinda, date.
    Habits of Mind: Struggling Over Values in America's
Classrooms / Melinda Fine. — 1st ed.
      p.   cm. — (The Jossey-Bass education series)
    Includes bibliographical references (p.   ) and index.
    ISBN 0-7879-0061-3 (alk. paper)
    1. Moral education—United States—Case studies.   2. Race
relations—Study and teaching—United States—Case studies.
3. Educational sociology—United States—Case studies.   4. Politics
and education—United States—Case studies.   5. Moral education—
Massachusetts—Cambridge. I. Title. II. Series.
LC311.F47   1995
370.11'4—dc20
                       94-41818
                       CIP

FIRST EDITION
HB Printing   10 9 8 7 6 5 4 3 2 1   Code 9517

The Jossey-Bass Education Series

For Zach and Talya, with
enormous thanks for the gift
of their love

Contents

Contents

Preface

Within the past two decades, American public education has become an increasingly important political issue. Many people have argued that our public schools are in deep trouble. Some point to the schools' seeming inability to turn out young people equipped with intellectual skills and a mastery of subjects traditionally deemed important. Others argue that schools are not taking advantage of their opportunity to impart moral values to students, pointing to alarming increases in acts of vandalism, violent assault, and bigotry committed by the young. And there has been much discussion about how schools can help an increasingly diverse student body deal with the conflicts and differences they encounter within and beyond school walls. These debates center around a fundamental question: What should our public schools be teaching and how should they be teaching it? Confronted with the fact of diversity, many educators now believe that America's public schools should help young people sort through today's many cultural, social, and political challenges. They call on schools to enhance their moral commitment to students by preparing them for an informed, principled engagement with the different communities and perspectives that make up the American democracy. This call has stirred a contentious debate that has deep roots in American history.

Much has been written about various aspects of this debate in the past several years. Some books use broad strokes to describe diverse programs that foster critical moral thinking, good character, and civic responsibility, while others focus more sharply on how specific programs are implemented in the classroom. This literature is illuminating, but it leaves some important gaps. Works that describe a range of programs are usually too broadly focused to shed much light on what happens once the programs are implemented in the classroom. Close-up studies often fail to assess what actually happens in the classroom in relation to public debates about what allegedly happens there. Those who argue from the policy arena frequently claim to know what is best for students, but they all too often lack contact with them in schools, where things are usually more subtle, complex, and ambiguous.

Habits of Mind moves the reader beyond the polemical and often caricatured arguments raised for or against programs to foster critical moral thinking, good character, and social responsibility in young people. Grounded in an in-depth study of the politics and practice of a single curriculum, it integrates a close-up look at the classroom with a broader discussion of educational theory and policy. It focuses on the nationally acclaimed yet politically controversial *Facing History and Ourselves* (FHAO) program, a course that uses a rigorous historical study of the Holocaust to guide students' critical reflection on contemporary racism, violence, intolerance, and prejudice. In exploring both how theoretical and policy arguments inform classroom dynamics and how classroom realities qualify theoretical positions, it gives a more nuanced portrayal of students' actual experience and a more accurate picture of the political issues at stake in this timely public debate.

Yet what I present here is more than a case study of a particular curriculum used in a single classroom, for the issues this book addresses are by no means unique to the FHAO program. The political influence of the New Right has been brought to bear not only against this program but against many other educational curricula and practices, while the values these students struggle over are broadly relevant in these times of contentious debate over diversity, national identity, and morality. As the writer Eudora Welty has noted in another context, "One place comprehended can make us understand other places better."

This book is conceived as a series of ever-widening lenses through which I view the politics and practice of curricula to foster critical moral thinking and social responsibility. The tightest lens looks at the classroom. It examines the daily practice of the Facing History and Ourselves curriculum in one multiracial middle school in Cambridge, Massachusetts. A second lens focuses on educational policy. It describes how FHAO and related educational programs fared during the Reagan era, when the New Right enjoyed heightened political influence. The widest lens provides a historical as well as an explicitly political perspective. It locates the issues raised by the Facing History and Ourselves case within American educational and political discourse more generally.

Overview of the Contents

The specific organization of the book is as follows. Chapter One, the introduction, presents a brief portrait of adolescents from the Boston area who have been brought together to discuss race relations. Through describing the conflicts and tensions illuminated by their discussion, I argue that young people are ready and eager to reckon with conflicting differences in American society, and that schools must prepare them to do so responsibly. The chapter also provides an overview of the Facing History and Ourselves curriculum.

The following three chapters describe classroom sessions in which the Facing History course engenders potentially conflictual differences among students. In this portion of the book, I look at how course pedagogy and materials help students deal with these differences. Chapter Two introduces the students, teacher, school, and community that ground this study and describes a lesson early on in the course where students began to define their "identity" in personal and social terms. Chapter Three looks at related class sessions later in the semester where differences in religious perspectives were brought to light. Chapter Four describes a series of classes toward the end of the course where contentious political differences

—in American society at large and in the microcosm of the class-room—were hotly debated.

The issues brought to light in these opening chapters are not unique to the Facing History curriculum. Chapter Five traces the history of programs to foster critical moral thinking and social responsibility in the schools and notes the struggles they engen-dered along the way. Beginning with the curricular reforms of Pro-gressive educators in the 1930s and 1940s, and ending with recent battles over "moral openness," "cultural literacy," and "multicul-turalism," the chapter argues that conflicts over educational vision, policy, and practice have always been linked to conflicts over com-peting visions of American democracy, its past, and its future.

Chapter Six situates these visions as they are manifested in the political arena by describing the increasing influence of New Right activists in matters of educational policy, particularly during the Reagan presidency. It analyzes the battle that ensued over federal funding for Facing History and Ourselves between 1986 and 1988. The chapter discusses how this controversy was framed alternatively by public policy makers, educators, New Right activists, and the media, thereby illuminating gaps and silences in public discourse on education in American society.

Chapter Seven, the conclusion, interprets the relationship between classroom practice, theory, and policy in light of the broader contemporary debate about dealing with difference in American society. I argue that promoting students' critical moral thinking is a vital responsibility of today's schools—a responsibil-ity essential to nurturing critical participatory democracy.

Goals and Methodology

Having briefly outlined what this book is about, I would like to make clear what it is not about. This book will not be tracing how the Facing History and Ourselves curriculum affected the beliefs of students over a long period of time, and it will not assess whether they in fact grew up to become active, responsible citizens. My focus is more immediate. I wanted to learn how students and their teacher interpreted issues raised by the Facing History course, and I assumed that these interpretations would shift throughout the semester, at times producing conflict among members of the class. I intended to describe how these conflicts were negotiated within the classroom. These concerns dictated a phenomenological and self-consciously personal approach to my subject. They required my daily presence in the classroom for an entire semester and my use of a variety of research methods, including participant observation, descriptive note-taking during class and analytical commentary notes after class, lengthy and at times repeated one-on-one interviews with students and their teacher, an interpretive reading of these interviews, and an ongoing review of all students' written work for the course. The classroom chapters of the book are a work of social science portraiture, designed to reveal dynamics and raise questions rather than to evaluate— or even to define—the curriculum's "success." As a matter of both research inquiry and writing style, portraiture investigates, describes, and analyzes characters, settings, and events in context, in relation to one another, keeping in mind the researcher's own relationship with his or her subject. Equally important, it seeks to engage the reader in the particular experience described in order to give him or her a sense of a larger whole.

This study is also deliberately grounded in one program's implementation in an urban, alternative middle school, and it does not presume to describe all critical moral thinking and social responsibility programs in all types of settings. I consider this focus an asset, because without having some hint of the million and one elements that go into putting any program in place—the school and community culture, the teacher, the students themselves, their parents' attitudes and beliefs, and more—we cannot understand how and why that program operates in that particular place in the way that it does. In fact, maybe we should be suspicious of authors who make grandiose claims in speaking for all students in all settings. These claims tend to obscure students' actual experience and are part of the problem with today's murky and highly politicized debates. On the other hand, I believe we can see a bigger picture by looking at things on a more micro level, because the issues that any single group of students wrestle with resonate in the different but not wholly dissimilar experiences of students in other settings, schools, and communities.

In writing on this topic, finally, I do not pretend to be a dispassionate, objective observer. Everyone speaks from some position, and rather than pretend that these positions do not exist, we need to make them as clear as possible. I am a strong supporter of the Facing History and Ourselves curriculum, and more generally of programs to foster critical moral thinking and social responsibility. I began doctoral work in education after working in the peace and feminist movements for a long time, and I came deliberately looking for models for developing social conscience in young people. I developed a professional collaboration with the Facing History and Ourselves curriculum early on in my doctoral studies, and that relationship has continued to grow over the past several years. I have observed and written on the program's implementation in a variety of middle and high schools in urban settings, and I have spoken at length with the program's teachers through my participation on the organization's national teacher training team.

This relationship has created opportunities as well as constraints, because by working closely with the organization, I have developed friendships with its teachers and staff and gained access to organizational files, staff meetings, and internal discussions. This access has deepened my understanding of the program, but at the same time it has demanded that I be vigilant in viewing its classroom practice in a fair and critical light. I identify where I stand in relation to this subject not to suggest that researcher "bias" undermines the validity of my observations—as if some wholly neutral position were a preferable point of departure, or even possible to attain. I believe all researchers stand in some relation to their subject; the reader simply deserves to know where I stand before I begin to describe and interpret these classroom events.

Intended Audience

This book has been written with several different but perhaps over-lapping audiences in mind. Readers with a general interest in education as an important arena of conflict in American politics and culture may find my discussion of the challenge of diversity within the educational domain particularly provocative. Teachers who are grappling with these kinds of issues every day in their classrooms may find it illuminating. Curriculum designers, educational administrators, policy makers, and activists, as well as those interested in the power and practice of the New Right, may be drawn to the book's discussion of Facing History's protracted battle in the policy arena during the Reagan years. And academics may wish to use the book in courses on moral development, educational policy and history, and curriculum design. Because the book employs ethnographic interpretive methods in the classroom, it may also be of use to those interested in qualitative research methods.

Acknowledgments

This book has been strengthened by the advice, assistance, and encouragement of many people, though its weaknesses are all my own. Sara Lawrence-Lightfoot, my adviser while I was at the Harvard Graduate School of Education, contributed greatly to the doctoral thesis out of which this book evolved. Her insights and criticism were particularly helpful in shaping my classroom portraits. Mary Moore, my close and lifelong friend, spent countless hours helping me conceptualize that earlier piece of work, and her continued support has sustained me throughout the revision process.

The staff, teachers, and students of Facing History and Ourselves have inspired me through the sometimes onerous process of turning my thesis into a book. I wish particularly to thank Marc Skvirsky, for his warmth and continued friendship; Margot Strom, for her vision and commitment to the issues of justice that underlie this curriculum; Steve Cohen, for his dynamic teaching and

humor; and Tracey O'Brien, for supplying me with countless necessary resources. I am greatly indebted to Kathy Greeley and
Yolanda Rodriguez, both excellent teachers who generously opened
up their classrooms to my prying eyes and ears. This book has been
shaped by the insights and concerns of many wonderful students. I
have used pseudonyms throughout the book to protect the
anonymity of these students, but the fact that they go unnamed
here does not mitigate the thanks I owe them all.

Many people helped directly or indirectly with particular parts
of this book. Nancy Murray of the Massachusetts Civil Liberties
Union spoke with me at length about the "Rap About Racism"
event I describe in Chapter One. The work of Carol Gilligan and
her colleagues contributed to the analysis of students' voices in
Chapter Two. Chip Berlet provided the resources and analytical
expertise of the Political Research Associates in Cambridge, Massachusetts, which strengthened my discussion of the New Right in
Chapters Five and Six. Herbert Kohl supplied useful information
about Harold Rugg's controversial social studies curriculum, which
I discuss in Chapter Five. And Max McConkey provided important
details about Facing History's battle for National Diffusion Network
(NDN) funding, which I address in Chapter Six.

I have been nourished by the encouragement and affection of
many wonderful friends and family members. Though they are too
numerous to name here, they know well their place in my heart.

The sudden death of my father-in-law, Michael Lockman, came
during the final months of my work on this project. Misha was an
exceptionally generous man whose commitment to helping those
in need was motivated in part by his own experience as a Holocaust
survivor. He came along with me one day as I observed one of the
classes I describe in this book; he was moved by the moral commitment of the Facing History course and was delighted by the
energy of its students. My respect for Misha bolsters my conviction
that educational programs like this are vital.

While working on this book, my life was blessed by the birth of
my daughter, Talya Mara Lockman-Fine. No words can capture the

joy this remarkable little girl has brought me over the past nineteen months. Though I might have finished this book sooner without her, I would have had less fun doing so. I have written this book with Talya in mind, in hopes that her future education will foster her own moral thinking, compassion, and action.

By far my greatest debt goes to my husband, Zachary Lockman, whose assistance on matters great and small helped shape whatever is of value in this book. Though busy writing a book of his own, he agreed to discuss this work with me time and time again, to read and reread every chapter, and to offer much-needed discerning criticism. What is worse, this poor man helped me just as much the first time around, when my work was still in thesis form. He has persevered because he loves me and believes in me; for this I feel extraordinarily lucky.

Boston, Massachusetts   MELINDA FINE
January 1995

Habits of Mind

Chapter One

Introduction: Fostering Democratic Habits of Mind

On a weekday morning in March 1990, several hundred middle and high school students from Boston and neighboring towns converged on the auditorium of the Massachusetts College of Art, on Boston's verdant Fenway, just across the street from the Museum of Fine Arts. The teenagers in the auditorium were a diverse group. There were black kids from schools in some of Boston's poor inner-city neighborhoods as well as white kids from middle-class and affluent suburban towns. And there was a racially and ethnically mixed group from Cambridge, just across the Charles River. Among them was a class of seventh and eighth graders from the Medgar Evers school.[1] I later talked a lot with these particular Cambridge students about what happened that day, and about much else besides; in fact, a good part of this book explores what happened in their classroom.

The students had been brought together for a "Rap About Racism" organized by the Massachusetts Civil Liberties Union and designed to encourage them to think about what the Bill of Rights might mean to them as its two hundredth anniversary approached. The program began smoothly enough. The students seemed happy to be with their friends on a field trip away from their schools. Most listened closely as adult speakers talked about racism in contemporary America and its historical context. But as the morning wore on, the program increasingly touched on issues that were closer to home, and on students' feelings about and attitudes toward people of other races. The audience erupted into sometimes heated argument after a group of black and white students from an alternative school in the Boston neighborhood of Dorchester performed a skit that depicted Boston police officers stopping people on the street and searching them.

What made the skit so provocative was the way it reversed traditional roles: the police officers were all black, while those stopped, frisked, and harassed were all white. This role reversal made many of the students, especially the white students, uneasy, and some were angered by what the skit seemed to be saying about who was an innocent victim and who was guilty of oppressive behavior. When the microphones were opened up for comments from the floor, the atmosphere quickly became heated and tense.

A white girl from the suburbs observed provocatively that blacks had only themselves to blame for police searches since they were the ones "bringing drugs into the country and killing each other and stuff." A black high school student countered that "white people have ruled this country for four hundred years, and they've messed up, so it's time for us to take over." A white middle school student told me later that "the black people in the audience were accusing white people, and the white people were just trying to defend their name." But others claimed that the white kids from the suburbs were ignorant, uninformed, or even racist.

Some of the black and white students from integrated schools— like the Cambridge middle schoolers I discussed the event with later—seemed to feel that their more heterogeneous school environment allowed them to have a better, less polarized perspective on race relations. But that did not mean that they felt easy about racial issues. The charged atmosphere at the Rap seemed to force people to take sides. One white girl who had been supportive of the blacks at the Rap later expressed confusion about her own racial identity. She told me, "The people I was siding with, they were talking about white people badly, but then that's like talking about me! I don't think they realized that they were talking about me, because they were really talking about the white racist people. But when they were trying to make them feel bad, they were making me feel bad, too. And it made me feel like, I'm for these people, but what do I think—that I'm black or something?"

A black classmate of hers also struggled with the question of how one's skin color was related to his or her point of view. She had been upset that a girl she assumed was biracial took the microphone and seemed to argue from what she perceived as an entirely "white" perspective that (as she later put it) "it was all the black people's— not the white people's—fault." She told me that right after the Rap had ended she had approached the girl who had spoken.

> I walked up to her later and I said, "Are you black or white?" And she said, "My father's black and my mother's white." So I said, "Well, why are you responding from the white point of view, and not looking at it from both sides?" And she said, "Well, I'm more white. I have lighter skin." And I said, "But, still." And she said, "Well, I just consider myself white." So I was like, "But you can't do that. You can't consider yourself white, and you can't consider yourself black, because you're mixed, so you should have mixed feelings on both sides!"

For most of the students who attended, the Rap About Racism seemed to evoke a complex set of emotions and questions about racial identity, about relationships across racial lines, even about the meaning of historical events. Race is one of the most painful and complex issues facing American society, evoking feelings that are difficult for Americans young and old to sort through and make sense of. It is not at all surprising that the discussion among the students at the Rap became so emotionally charged so quickly.

That it was a skit about the police stopping and searching people on the street that initially brought racial tensions to the surface also makes sense, for the Rap took place just a few months after Boston had been shocked by a bizarre and racially charged murder that had prompted the Boston police to carry out large-scale search operations in apparent disregard of the civil rights of innocent black men.[2] This case dominated the headlines for months, and it cannot have been far from the minds of the students attending the Rap About Racism on that March day in 1990. It probably made the police-search skit put on by the students from Dorchester seem particularly provocative and the ensuing discussion more heated.

Those who witnessed the Rap About Racism had differing views about the event's usefulness. One *Boston Globe* reporter, in a story published under the headline "Shouts Drown Out Rap at Youth Racism Forum," took a negative view and argued that the program had moved dangerously beyond "scripted events."[3] Some students apparently agreed; one told me that "it was just a bunch of yelling and arguing. Instead of trying to solve racism, which we thought was the purpose, it made people more angry." "I didn't expect it to turn out like this," another girl remarked. "I expected it to be educational."

But a member of the Massachusetts Civil Liberties Union staff who had organized the Rap took issue with these negative appraisals. She argued that most students were able to listen to each other despite—or perhaps even because of—the intense passions aroused. And many students shared these sentiments. One commented, "People got out what they were feeling more when they got all worked up. I bet if it had been with all adults they wouldn't have said those things, they would have hid their feelings. At least here they got them out! And I wanted to hear what they were." Another student remarked, "It was really interesting to hear different points of view from a different race. I know what black people are saying about this, but it's more interesting to see what some white people might be saying instead of just my point of view."

Regardless of whether one judges the Rap a success or a failure, it does tell us one important thing: teenagers are aware of and engaged with what is going on around them, not just regarding highly charged racial issues but regarding many other issues as well. The minds of the kids who walked into the auditorium where the Rap was held were not blank slates; they were filled with a host of attitudes and images and feelings and ideas. Adolescents may not always think about social issues or articulate them in the ways that the media or politicians or their parents do, but they are not unaware of them, and they are often eager to discuss them with their peers. Moreover, the ways they engage with these issues are often inextricably bound up with the issues of personal identity and social development they face as adolescents, and therefore are felt with a special intensity.

This engagement is often tempestuous and difficult, and students in this age group may have very different, even conflicting, opinions and attitudes, and very different capacities for becoming clear about their own stance and its implications and consequences. Whatever else the Rap may have accomplished, it demonstrated that adolescents need help in becoming more informed about the issues at stake, help in getting clearer about their own attitudes and beliefs, and help in learning to listen to each other so they can deal respectfully with those who think and feel differently. Since school is a place where students spend many hours each day interacting with others, and since it is a place devoted to instilling not only knowledge but also habits of mind, it must be one of the places where students are helped to deal productively with these kinds of conflicts and differences. As adult citizens of a democracy, they will be called on to contend with different viewpoints and make morally significant choices, whether at the ballot box or in their everyday lives. It seems reasonable that as the key institution to which a democratic society entrusts the formation of its youth, schools can and should play a role in instilling democratic habits of mind in today's young people.

Like all important goals, this is of course easier said than done. And there is no doubt that passions may be aroused along the way. But as the organizer of the Rap About Racism put it, "My hope was to get kids thinking, and to get teachers thinking. Even if they felt challenged by it or worried by it, I wanted at least to wake them up! Racism is an incredibly painful topic, and had we had that conference without producing pain, it would have meant that we did not get near the heart of the problem. The question is: Do you deal with the issue, recognizing that pain will be a part of it? Or do you just decide not to, to avoid the pain?"

Today's adolescents, like the rest of us, live in an increasingly complicated and diverse society, a society facing challenges that produce considerable social, political, and cultural contention. There is no way to suppress or avoid that contention, at least not within a democratic framework. I argue that one must instead accept it as a reality and try to equip tomorrow's citizens with the skills and habits of mind that will help them decide who they are, what they believe, and what they must do as active and responsible participants in the American democracy.

Struggling Over Values in the Classroom

Over the past several years, literally hundreds of educational programs have been developed for just this purpose. Instilling "good values" in children has been part of the educational agenda since the early days of American schooling. But today's almost feverish interest in what can be most broadly defined as "values education" reflects a concern that children and young adults be better prepared to deal with the conflicts and challenges born of diversity, in the hope that this may help reverse numerous troubling signs of civil decay—among them the escalation of acts of murder, violent assault, and vandalism committed disproportionately by young people, and the growing incidence of hate crimes and other acts of bigotry, again perpetrated increasingly by the young.

In some instances, these educational initiatives have been embedded within students' "basic" school subjects, like history or English; in others, they occupy a distinct place within the school curriculum. The programs go by different names and emphasize different things, though common impulses unite them. Since I will mention several different initiatives in this book, it may be helpful to define my terms briefly at the outset.

Programs committed to *moral education* seek to develop ethical values and behaviors in students. Many emphasize moral reasoning, focusing on the child's capacity to recognize what is morally at issue in a given situation and to make morally informed choices in resolving conflicts. A task force of nationally prominent educators convened in 1988 by the Association for Supervision and Curriculum Development, a professional organization devoted to "developing leadership for quality in education," proposed six distinct characteristics of a "morally mature" person that programs should seek to foster. These are: showing respect for human dignity (which includes promoting human equality and working with people of different views); caring about the welfare of others (which includes seeking social justice as well as caring for one's country); integrating individual interests and social responsibilities; demonstrating integrity; reflecting on moral choices; and seeking the peaceful resolution of conflict (which includes listening carefully to others and working for peace).[4] Moral education programs may also go under the name of *character education*, though character-oriented initiatives may focus more specifically on developing certain socially valued traits, attitudes, and behaviors in individuals—for example, honesty, kindness, generosity, perseverance, respect, and tolerance. Character education programs flourished in the 1920s and 1930s and have taken on renewed urgency in the 1990s.

While both moral and character education programs have existed in some form or other since the early days of common schooling, multicultural, antiracist, and conflict resolution programs are more recent phenomena, the products of both the opportunities and the tensions born of America's changing demographics and other social, cultural, and political trends. *Multicultural* curricula seek to sensitize students to the fact of cultural diversity by teaching about the histories and cultures of different ethnic groups. *Antiracist* curricula take the additional step of investigating the history of unequal power relations among these groups. They seek to sharpen students' awareness of prejudice and bigotry and strengthen their resolve to act against them. Programs in *conflict resolution* and *violence prevention* help students find ways to resolve conflicts peacefully, without resorting to verbal or physical violence. They often advance an intellectual predisposition toward nonviolence and teach specific interpersonal skills like peer mediation and counseling.

Certain pedagogical priorities underlie these varied initiatives. Since "good" actions are premised on the individual's ability to know right from wrong and to behave accordingly, many programs teach *critical thinking* skills to nurture each student's development of his or her own moral compass. Throughout much of American history, educators favored indoctrinating methods as a way of instilling moral standards in children, and we will see later that some still favor these approaches. However, most moral educators now stress the importance of the student's own capacity to reflect critically on issues confronted. In this respect, the methodology of the various curricula described above is in step with a growing educational trend to foster critical thinking in many other parts of the curriculum.

Instilling positive moral values in schoolchildren sounds good; raising engaged, socially responsible future citizens sounds even better. But these seemingly straightforward goals raise complex questions: What values are to be deemed positive? By whose authority are they to be promoted? How should they be taught in schools? What is their relation to the schools' many other functions and responsibilities? These questions have always plagued moral and social responsibility initiatives, and as a consequence, such programs have always been hotly contested.

Moreover, though these questions concern education most directly, they are inextricably bound up with social and cultural issues more generally. For education has long been seen as central not only to individual character formation but also to the shaping of who we are as a nation and where we are going. As a result, debates over the mission, content, and methods of public education in the United States have usually involved conflicting visions of American identity, of the character of the society we live in, and of how differences and cleavages within that society should be dealt with. Conversely, many of the key social, political, and cultural issues that Americans have fought over have also resonated in, and often affected, the educational arena.

As we will see, there are those who argue that public schools should not seek to inculcate moral reasoning and critical thinking skills in students. They oppose spending classroom time on teaching students how to clarify, express, and argue for their beliefs, contending instead that schools should stick to promoting "basic" intellectual skills and mastery of certain subjects. These critics generally range from the conservative to the far-right end of the political spectrum. They envision America as a unified entity in which differences in gender, race, class, ethnicity, and sexual orientation are secondary, if not irrelevant, and must be transcended. As a consequence, they regard curricula that sensitize students to difference as divisive, indeed as potential threats to the social glue that holds a democratic society together. They insist that those who promote these programs are in fact indoctrinating children with their own partisan liberal agenda. While these arguments date back to the Progressive education reforms of the 1930s and 1940s, they took on renewed urgency with the growth of the New Right in the 1980s and 1990s.

I believe that arguing that schools should stick solely to the "basics" is in fact a dodge. Conservative and New Right critics are not really against schools imparting moral and political values to students; they are simply against imparting values they consider "wrong." Their opposition to fostering critical moral thinking stems from their desire to impart their own values to young people—values they implicitly or explicitly claim are authentic, unchanging, and truly "American."

Advocates of curricula to instill critical moral thinking and social responsibility also appeal to an apolitical ideal. They argue that their curricula espouse values such as tolerance for difference and respect for diversity—values they also regard as "American" to their core. But in reality, these purportedly apolitical "prosocial" values are also bound up with a particular vision of America, one that tends to see America as a diverse and pluralistic society. This perspective takes note of real, and often conflicting, differences in viewpoints and interests among various social groups. And it sees democracy as being about establishing the processes whereby these conflicts can be played out, issues clarified and debated fully, and mechanisms established that ensure that social groups who are differently positioned gain equal access to society's goods.

Both educational visions reflect a vision of America, but the visions are different, and that difference is political. In arguing for or against programs to encourage "character," "moral growth," and "social responsibility," neither side can fairly appeal to a politically neutral, universally agreed-on vision of America or of its values, history, or future. No such thing exists. Instead, we must accept and embrace the fact that diversity and difference exist in both the composition of this country and the way its citizens conceive of it. Only from this vantage point can we focus on ways of reckoning with that difference, so we can make the debate about who we are and where we are going more productive and fruitful.

The Facing History and Ourselves Curriculum

This book provides an in-depth study of a curriculum that has been at the center of debates about moral thinking and social responsibility curricula. Developed in 1976 by middle school teachers in Brookline, Massachusetts, the *Facing History and Ourselves* (FHAO) curriculum seeks to provide a model for teaching history in a way that helps adolescents reflect critically on a variety of contemporary social, moral, and political issues. It focuses on a specific historical period—the Nazi rise to power and the Jewish Holocaust—and guides students back and forth between an in-depth historical case study and reflection on the causes and consequences of present-day prejudice, intolerance, violence, and racism. The program reaches nearly half a million students a year in rural, urban, and suburban settings in public, private, and parochial schools. Through its national headquarters in Brookline and its satellite offices in Chicago, Los Angeles, Memphis, and New York, the FHAO organization has trained a nationwide network of some 30,000 educators to teach the program.

In the context of today's increasing attention to multicultural issues, Facing History's decision to use the Holocaust as a spring-

board for exploring contemporary issues may require some expla-
nation. When the program was created by teachers in the late
1970s, relatively few Holocaust curricula existed. Perceiving the
Holocaust to be a watershed event of the twentieth century, these
teachers felt strongly that their students should learn about such a
critical episode in modern history. At the same time, they felt that
the Holocaust's "meaning" must lie not only in understanding its
unique historical dimensions, but also in grappling with its more
generalizable lessons about human behavior. Historically examining the escalation of steps through which German citizens came to
follow Hitler—from the uses of propaganda to influence one's
thinking, to the threats against one's economic and personal security, to the uses of terror to compel obedience—course designers
sought to help students identify how opportunities for resistance
were eroded with the demise of German democracy and the rise of
a totalitarian state. Using historical understanding as a catalyst for
a more critical and personal reflection, they intended to facilitate
students' ability to recognize how they themselves respond when
faced with group pressure to conform. They also sought to foster
their awareness of the societal conditions that can constrain or
destroy democratic freedoms (whether in a contemporary or historical context), and to highlight avenues for civic responsibility to
protect democratic mechanisms against these developments.

It might well be asked whether these goals could not also be
achieved by undertaking a different, perhaps more relevant case
study—of the Middle Passage, for example, or the genocide of
Native Americans. No doubt they could be. Program designers,
teachers, and promoters do not argue that the Holocaust is the only
genocide—or even the most important genocide—to teach about.[5]
But they do contend that discussions about contemporary racism
and violence may in fact be facilitated by focusing on a period of
history more tangential to the cultural backgrounds of the course's
ethnically diverse students. As the director of an inner-city high
school in Boston that teaches the Facing History course remarked,
the program offers "a way to talk about these issues in a *removed* way

so that we don't hit people over the head with a two-by-four and say 'racism!' 'scapegoating!'"[6]

In keeping with Facing History's educational priorities, the semester-long curriculum is structured to move back and forth between a focus on "history" and a focus on "ourselves." Initial chapters of the program's *Resource Book* encourage thinking about universal questions of individual identity and social behavior. From here, the course moves on to its more specific case study of prejudice and discrimination: an examination of the history of anti-semitism, beginning as far back as ancient Rome. Students undertake a rigorous and multifaceted study of German history from 1914 to 1945, examining, for example, the impact of Nazi racial policies in education and the workplace, the nature of propaganda, and the various roles played by victims, victimizers, and bystanders during the period of the Third Reich. These lessons not only provide critical historical content, but also serve as structured exercises for thinking about the choices that individuals, groups, and nations faced with regard to action and resistance. These exercises, in turn, prepare students for later discussions about how one judges those who perpetrated or were silently complicit in the Holocaust, and about how students themselves can assume responsibility for protecting civil liberties and becoming active citizens of a democracy.[7]

Facing History's complex intellectual content is undergirded by a pedagogical imperative: to foster perspective taking, critical thinking, and moral decision making among students. It is specifically geared toward adolescents who are developmentally engaged in a fierce (and somewhat contradictory) struggle to become distinct individuals *and* to fit in with their peers. These students, curriculum developers argue, have the most to gain from a course that "raises the problem of differing perspectives, competing truths, the need to understand motives and to consider the intentions and abilities of themselves and others."[8] Rather than shying away from the conflicts that are inevitably generated as a diverse group of adolescents work to clarify their own beliefs and values, program participants are encouraged to view complexity and conflict as potentially conducive to personal growth and democratic citizenship.

These are admittedly controversial ideas, and precisely because Facing History tackles them head on, the curriculum became a target of New Right opposition to critical moral education initiatives in the 1980s. Under the leadership of New Right organizer Phyllis Schlafly and with the unflagging assistance of Ronald Reagan's political appointees within the Department of Education, the Facing History and Ourselves organization was repeatedly denied federal funding to disseminate the curriculum between 1986 and 1988. For reasons that we will explore later, the funding denials sparked congressional hearings and heated debate among public policy makers, educators, and other concerned citizens; these debates drew substantial media attention.

The public controversy surrounding funding for Facing History fundamentally concerned different—and competing—visions of America, democracy, patriotism, and citizenship. It reveals how different groups (in this case, the FHAO organization, members of Congress, activists in the New Right, Jewish organizations, government officials, and members of the press) have different understandings of what should be taught in American schools and who should make that decision. More significantly, it reveals a lack of social consensus around how public education should address the fact of difference in American society. Recognizing this lack of a shared consensus, individuals across the political spectrum compete to define America's educational purpose and mission. In this instance as well as historically, they conflict on both cultural and political ground. The Facing History and Ourselves funding controversy presents an excellent case study for examining the politics surrounding educational programs to promote critical moral thinking and social responsibility in the schools.

This curriculum is also exceptionally well suited for a close-up look at how these programs are put into practice in the classroom, because it crosses some of the intellectual and ideological boundaries that may otherwise hinder discussion of a particular program's merits or shortcomings. Facing History integrates many of the concerns of the kinds of educational initiatives already described: it uses critical thinking pedagogy to foster good character and moral growth; it seeks to build civic-mindedness and democratic citizenship; it promotes social responsibility by encouraging antiracist and nonviolent thinking; and it grounds this multifaceted project in the concrete subject matter of history. The program is one of twenty-one programs or organizations selected to be part of a National Network of Violence Prevention Practitioners, and it plays a growing role in the school reform movement, collaborating with restructuring initiatives such as the Coalition for Essential Schools and the New American Schools Development Corporation. By stressing Facing History's "connectedness," I do not mean to suggest that it equally represents each and every program that falls under the "values education" net. But by integrating diverse new approaches, it shows us what some of these initiatives have in common, particularly with regard to the controversy they have engendered. And by teaching critical moral thinking through the lessons of history, it proves that educational basics and values education can go hand in hand.

To see how all of this gets done, we must visit the classroom and hear what the students have to say.

Part One

Classroom Portraits

Chapter Two

"What Makes
You You?"

There is a ten-minute break between math and social studies class. Students are everywhere, noisy and active. Everybody seems to be eating: chocolate chip cookies, Hostess Ho Ho's, Reese's peanut butter cups, and at least one banana. Lunch is not for another hour, and these twelve- and thirteen-year-old students are hungry.

Angela and Sandra play Ping-Pong in the back of the room on the white Formica table that serves as a work space when class is in session. Jamal, Amiri, and Abby sit around the table and cheer them on. Jamal, the reigning Ping-Pong champion from the last classroom break, tilts back in his chair to keep a running tally on the chalkboard. Unabashedly praising herself for each point she makes, Sandra, a tall, skinny white girl, is easily beating Angela, a soft-spoken black Jamaican American who is taking it good-humoredly, though she seems a bit embarrassed.

Nearby, in the corner of the room usually reserved for morning meetings, two white girls sit cross-legged on flattened pillows and talk. Melody and Kyle appear intimate, and they giggle a lot. Their familiarity is matched by the warm tone of this "meeting corner"— a few plaid couch cushions border one side of an old blue rug; a stack of board games fills two cubicles of modular shelving; an American flag hangs over one door, while a poster of the earth as seen from space is taped to another.

A few feet away, Chi-Ho and Zeke continue a game of chess they have begun earlier in the morning. Absorbed and intent, they seem an unlikely pair. Chi-Ho, a thin Chinese boy who has been in the United States just a year and a half, wears conservative gray slacks, a pressed, beige cotton shirt buttoned at both the neck and cuffs, and thick black-rimmed glasses. By contrast, Zeke is relaxed and disheveled. His sleek blond hair hangs in a loose ponytail several inches down his back, and his oversized sweater and chino pants drape over his slim, tightly muscled body. The two boys chuckle and rib each other between chess moves; though their styles are different, their comfortable rapport is readily apparent.

Several other students walk freely around the room. Yoshi, Mandy, Duane, and Tyrone each sit by themselves, doodling or reading. Josh and Alan, two white boys with marginally punk hairdos, laugh at something in Josh's desk. Marlene, a striking black girl who works as a model on weekends, puts something in one of the wooden coat lockers that line one wall of the classroom. Two brothers from Korea, Bok Joon and Hee Joon, chase each other out the door and down the hall.

Marysa Gonzales is the teacher of these students. She searches intently through piles of paper on her desk, undisturbed by the constant, lively clatter of shouting and laughter. She seems not to notice the Ping-Pong ball as it skids off the game table and pops across the linoleum floor. A handsome Latina in her late forties, Marysa's style is informal and unpretentious: she wears a loose-fitting black cotton shirt, gray wool slacks, and no makeup. Her long black hair is pulled back in a loose braid and streaked with gray.

A new visitor to the classroom, I am struck by how relaxed, socially integrated, and simply fun this place seems to be. Students of different races and ethnicities apparently choose to play together during free time; some social groupings even cross the divide of gender. It is February, and this is the beginning of the second semester of the school year. Marysa informs me that the integration I see reflects five months of concerted effort: "It's something we've been working very, very hard to develop."

The Community

In large part, the classroom's diversity reflects that of the city of Cambridge, Massachusetts, in which it is situated. Just across the

Charles River from Boston, this 350-year-old city is perhaps best known for its rich academic heritage: it is the home of Harvard University and the Massachusetts Institute of Technology (MIT). Outsiders generally envision Cambridge as a white, middle-class, intellectual enclave, and these perceptions are at least partially true.

Harvard University sits in the center of the densely populated 6.2-square-mile town. Its ivy-covered, colonial red brick buildings, white painted steeples, and expansive green commons bustling with students are so synonymous with the popular image of the New England Ivy League that they appear almost a cliché. Outside the wrought-iron gates of Harvard Yard, the Harvard Square business district teems with well-stocked bookstores, crowded coffee houses, upscale clothing boutiques, and myriad gourmet shops selling cheeses and canned goods, natural cosmetics, and home-made ice cream. Winding along tree-lined Brattle Street out of Harvard Square, tourists often come to ogle Cambridge's large, well-kept colonial homes, many dating back to the 1700s. Once nicknamed "Tory Row," these stately mansions with their manicured lawns and wrap-around porches, white Doric columns, and shingled roofs embody the affluence, prestige, and historic presence so often associated with the university and its environs.

But Brattle Street represents only one of thirteen distinct neighborhoods in this densely packed city of almost 100,000. While a substantial portion of the town's residents are middle- to upper-income (the median family income of city residents was $40,000 in 1989), 45 percent of city residents earn low or moderate incomes (under $36,000 for a family of four), and 7 percent live below the poverty line. Over the past two decades, the city has lost much of its light manufacturing base. Now nearly two-thirds of all local jobs are in education, health, and business services. Harvard and MIT, Polaroid, Lotus Development, Mt. Auburn Hospital, and MIT's Draper Labs are the city's largest employers. Those who perceive Cambridge as having become increasingly "yuppified" in recent years can point to the fact that almost half of its residents now work in professional and managerial positions. Thirty-one percent work in technical, sales, and clerical positions; 11 percent work in a ser-vice capacity; and 11 percent are in blue-collar trades.

Though these figures are significant, city demographics are in fact in flux. While the overall urban population has been in decline (the 1990 census reports Cambridge's population is 95,802, which is down from a peak of 120,740 in 1950), the percentage of minorities in the city (largely immigrant and low-income) has been increasing. In 1990, Cambridge residents were 72 percent white, 13 percent black, 8 percent Asian, and 7 percent Hispanic; this represents a 40 percent increase in Cambridge's minority pop-ulation and an 8 percent decrease in its white population over the previous decade.

Cambridge's increasing minority presence is largely due to the influx of new immigrants to the city. One-fifth of all Cambridge res-idents are foreign-born, and one-half of these arrived between 1980 and 1990. Most came from Cape Verde, Brazil, Southeast Asia, Central America, and Haiti. Residents under eighteen are even more racially diverse than the city as a whole, probably because many immigrants are young and the white population has a lower birthrate. The city's under-eighteen population is 60 percent white, 26 percent black, 8 percent Asian, and 6 percent other minorities. In fact, since many new immigrants are undocumented aliens, cen-sus figures probably underestimate the actual number of Cam-bridge's nonwhite and foreign-born residents.

New immigrants tend to reside in neighborhoods far different from the city's more affluent quarters, though they are not far apart in terms of physical distance. Following Massachusetts Avenue east out of Harvard Square, one sees fewer impeccable tree-lined streets and more black, brown, and yellow faces. Homes become smaller, more crowded together, and often more run-down. The majority of Haitians and Hispanics and, to a lesser extent, Cape Verdeans and West Indians live just north of Massachusetts Avenue, toward East Cambridge and the neighboring town of Somerville. This area has the highest poverty level in the city (in 1990, 19 percent of the families in this area lived below the poverty line, more than double the citywide average) and it lags behind the city average in educational level as well. Central Americans and other Latinos, Asians, West Indians, and Haitians also reside in the neighborhoods of Cambridgeport and Riverside, just south of Massachusetts Avenue toward the river, where black residents comprise 19 percent of the population. These neighborhoods, too, are poorer than the city as a whole.[1]

The School

The racial and ethnic diversity of Cambridge's population and the vast socioeconomic differences among its neighborhoods have implications for Cambridge public schools. The city's fourteen primary schools and one comprehensive high school are attended by some 8,000 students from more than four dozen countries of origin. Their families speak forty-six different languages; just over 25 percent speak a language other than English at home. A plethora of innovative programs are offered throughout these schools to meet students' diverse needs. One school houses an integrated Spanish/English program; another, a bilingual program for Creole-speaking Haitian immigrants; yet another, a bilingual program for Southeast Asians. Programs for "academically talented" pupils and for those requiring special education exist in different settings, and a variety of "alternative" programs are housed within schools offering, among other things, Follow Through/Magnet Programs, a computer-oriented curriculum, and open classrooms emphasizing academic creativity and strong parental involvement.

Atypical of public education trends over the past decade, Cambridge schools are well funded. In 1990, the city spent $7,395 on every pupil in its system—50 percent more than the national average. The school's solid fiscal base comes in large part from Cambridge residents who in 1981 voted to override Proposition 2½, a successful statewide ballot measure that capped real estate taxes and resulted in massive school personnel layoffs and school program reductions in other parts of the state.

Parental involvement in Cambridge public schools is in a sense mandated by the city's Controlled Choice School Assignment Plan. The first of its kind in the nation, Cambridge instituted this districtwide initiative in 1981 as the final phase of a voluntary school desegregation plan. After the federal courts required desegregation of the Boston public schools in the mid 1970s, the Massachusetts State Department of Education required that schools throughout the state not be racially "imbalanced." "Imbalanced" schools were defined as those having over 50 percent minority students. Hoping to avoid the turmoil and violence that accompanied court-ordered school desegregation in Boston, Cambridge officials solicited grassroots participation in the design of an effective and fair plan for the city's fourteen primary schools. Over the course of several years, city officials put into effect a multistage plan designed to provide free transportation for all children who needed it; develop and retain a multiethnic school staff and faculty; and ensure a child's ability to stay within a given school once she or he was placed there, to the greatest extent possible.

According to the plan, parents are invited to list at least three choices for a school assignment for their children. Placement determinations are to be based on criteria that include the impact on the school's racial balance, space availability, sibling preference (those with a sibling already in a given school are given priority), and proximity of the child's home to the school of choice. As described by the Cambridge School Committee's Controlled Choice School Assignment Plan, the goal of the program is

> to graduate from our high school young adults who have pride in themselves, who respect and accept others as equals, and who are confident of their ability to work with and get along with whomever they meet, without either fear or arrogance. . . . The children of Cambridge are fortunate that, within its public school system, the city can provide a foretaste of that diverse world they will inhabit. Our schools include children from many different cultures, many nations, speaking many languages. Desegregation was the first step

in a process that enabled children to take advantage of that diversity. . . . Together they have learned about themselves and each other, about the world as it has been, as it is today, and as it might be in the future. Their teachers continue to learn how to use the diversity of the city and its students in developing a multicultural approach to education.[2]

Because of grassroots involvement in planning and the extensive efforts made to inform the Cambridge public, the city's Controlled Choice Plan went smoothly into effect in 1981, and now all fourteen of Cambridge's primary schools have achieved racial balance. Parents continue to be highly involved in the choice process, with two out of three parents visiting various primary schools before selecting their schools of choice. However, Cambridge School Department Public Information Director Bert Giroux notes that parents look for different things when choosing schools and that these differences have an impact on school composition: "The parents with a higher educational background usually choose the more open and flexible academic programs, while bilingual parents and those living in the projects tend to look for proximity. They want schools that are closer to home." As a result, many white, middle-class parents complain of not being able to get their children into the programs they want (a case of too many white children competing for too few slots), and poor and/or immigrant students tend to remain clumped in the schools situated in low-income neighborhoods. For example, 65 percent of the students attending Harrington (a school in a heavily immigrant neighborhood) meet federal guidelines entitling them to free or reduced-price lunches, as compared to only 17 percent of the students attending Agassiz, a school close to Harvard and the more affluent parts of the city.[3]

Marysa Gonzales's students attend the Medgar Evers school, which is located in one of the poorer neighborhoods of the city. Here primarily black, Latino, Haitian, and Asian families live in multifamily homes. Unlike the well-kept, white-trimmed mansions near Harvard University, houses near Medgar Evers are usually close together and are often in need of paint or new siding. Many of Medgar Evers's students come from the large housing project just across the street; 44 percent of the school qualifies for free or reduced-price lunches. Because of the city's desegregation program, however, the school's roughly 600 K–8 students are more racially balanced than the neighborhood in which the school is located: in 1992–93, the school was 43 percent white, 34 percent African American, 16 percent Asian, and 7 percent Hispanic.

Medgar Evers is a long, three-story beige concrete building of irregular geometric design. Surrounded by few trees, the school appears cold and austere when viewed from the street. Inside, however, one gets an entirely different impression. Classrooms, offices, the school library, and the auditorium spin off from an airy central space that is open from the third floor to the basement. Sunlight streams in through skylights on the school's slanted roof, infusing all three floors of the building with light. Terracotta-tiled floors, clean hallways, notices for bake sales and other school events, as well as abundant displays of student artwork, make the school feel cheery and welcoming. A long, student-painted mural stretches down one wall of the main floor's central space. Each of the mural's brightly painted panels contains a distinct cultural image: a village scene from Ghana; a scene of Medgar Evers pointing to the school, with black and white children playing together outside it; women in Bangladesh; children playing in Seoul, Korea; bagpipers from Scotland. An enormous map of the world hangs on an adjacent wall, just across from the school's central office. The map is covered with pushpins, each connected to a string that leads to a flag representing the country pinpointed. "We have children and families in our school representing *at least* 64 countries of the world," a card next to the map states. "We want to encourage children to become familiar with the world map, to identify all of the countries of origin, and to help celebrate our diversity!"

Like many primary schools throughout Cambridge, Medgar Evers houses a variety of programs for bilingual, special education, and mainstream students. Most students belong to one of the school's autonomous programs run under the direction of one principal and vice-principal. These programs differ significantly in terms of pedagogy, curriculum, and management.

Initiated by parents and offered as an educational option by the School Department since 1975, the Medgar Evers "Open Program" stresses a multicultural curriculum, a flexible, activity-centered learning environment, multigraded classrooms, critical thinking pedagogy, and strong parent participation in many aspects of teaching, administration, and fundraising. According to Jane Edmonds, the school's vice-principal, the program's primary goal is "to teach kids how to live in a pluralistic society, to help them acknowledge that this *is* a very pluralistic society, and to give credibility and credence to the contributions of other cultures and ethnic groups and attention to the role they've played in world history."

Evers's older "Regular Program" follows a more traditional educational model. Emphasizing basic intellectual skills and a less multicultural focus, Regular Program teachers are more oriented toward formal, teacher-directed instructional styles than toward "peer teaching, cooperative teams, and student-managed learning." Some members of the Regular community have even urged the program to change its name—from the ambiguous "Regular" to the more forceful "Academy for Traditional Studies."

Though the Regular Program has roughly one-third more students than the Open Program, its teachers complain that a disproportionate amount of resources go to the school's Open half. Major struggles between the two programs have been brewing for years around a host of equity issues. According to Edmonds, these include conflicts over how school resources should be allocated; perceptions on the part of Regular Program staff that the Open Program gets more money, more access to materials and supplies, and more parent involvement; and frustration (again on the part of Regular staff) that the middle-class parents who are usually associated with the Open Program are more able to contribute to school than the working-class parents usually associated with "Regular." "Regular Program staff see the Open teachers and parents as pushy and aggressive," Edmonds explains. "They feel intimidated, put out, and put upon by Open staff." While Edmonds sympathizes with these sentiments, she also notes that Regular suffers from having a less cohesive staff than the Open Program and from being less clear about its goals and priorities. She suggests that they must learn to work together "better as a group" to get "clearer about what they want" and "more assertive in going after it."

Marysa Gonzales teaches in the Open Program. Her classroom includes twenty-three students in grades seven and eight. Of the twelve girls and eleven boys in this class, six are African-American, four are Asian, and thirteen are white, one of whom is a Latina. Many of these students have been in the Open Program since kindergarten. A few newcomers to the school landed here by chance through the workings of the school assignment system. By contrast, Hee Joon and Bok Joon chose to transfer in from the Regular Program, where they felt picked on because of their race and lack of good English. No longer teased or made to feel different, they feel more welcome here. While all these students seem to enjoy what the Open Program has to offer, their understanding of its difference from Regular appears more pragmatic than philosophical. "When I first came here," Marysa explains, "I asked students to tell me what being in the Open Program was all about. They said it just means that your classroom has a rug and a couch in it, and that you can call your teacher by her first name."

The Curriculum

I am here for the first week of the new interdisciplinary social studies unit, "Facing History and Ourselves." Students have been told that they will learn about the Holocaust, and they have spent the past two days discussing what that might entail. Today's lesson comes from an opening chapter of the curriculum's *Resource Book*, a dense text designed for use by both teachers and students. Surprisingly, this chapter does not begin by introducing the

Holocaust as a subject of study. Instead, it raises universal questions about human values, beliefs, and behaviors, asking students to explore issues of identity in both personal and sociological terms. Students are encouraged to think about how one's values are formed, what social factors influence one's beliefs, and how social conditions can both enable and constrain acting on what one believes in.

Titled "Society and the Individual," the chapter posits individuals as decision makers within a social context who wrestle with the sometimes conflicting demands of loyalty, obedience, and social responsibility. In keeping with the curriculum's developmental focus, this chapter of the *Resource Book* speaks to adolescents' somewhat contradictory yearnings both to become distinct individuals *and* to "fit in" with social groups and be accepted by their peers. Themes raised in this chapter are intended to serve as a foundation for the specific historical study that will follow. In later sections, students will examine a constellation of social, cultural, and political factors creating conditions in which individuals chose to follow fascist doctrine, or, far less often, to resist it. As the *Resource Book* explains, "In this chapter students are introduced to the concept of the role of the individual in society. Students develop working definitions for the terms *society* and *individual*, and brainstorm those aspects of society such as family, religion, political groups, school, grade, friends, race, town, city, state, nation, and values which contribute to the individual's identity."[4]

A variety of exercises and curricular readings facilitate this intellectual and personal study. Early on, for example, students are asked to construct "identity charts" that diagram elements they consider essential to their identity. In answer to Marysa's question "What makes you *you?*" students write their name in the middle of a sheet of paper and draw a circle around it. From this circle they extend lines out in all directions, labeling each line with a different quality, personal characteristic, or social factor they consider important to their sense of self. What emerges are an abundance of diagrams rich in data about students' habits and hobbies, likes and dislikes, friends and family, ethnic and racial characteristics, and religious affiliations. Identity charts become topics of discussion among members of the classroom community and subjects for ongoing personal reflection. Throughout the course, a student may ask, "How does being black affect how I see myself and am seen by others?" or "How do my parents' values influence how I make sense of the world?"

The students and teachers are offered a variety of resources to facilitate answering questions such as these. A dystopia short story by Kurt Vonnegut presents a future society in which universal conformity has been mandated by law. A children's story describes a tragicomedy in which a bear, despite his remonstrations, is mistaken for a human being and forced to live in a human world because others refuse to see him for what he is. A film presents a parable in which an adolescent struggles with conflicting family values and the demands of growing up.

This morning Marysa chooses to show her students the resource film. Classroom break time is over, and she reconvenes class by making a series of announcements referring to other units in the year's social studies curriculum: "The westward expansion group will be performing today. The women's suffrage group and the immigration group also need to meet." A few pairs of friends hang back and continue talking, while others go quickly to their seats. As students begin to settle down, Marysa hands out the first-week syllabus of the Facing History course. Some look over what will be expected of them in the week ahead—numerous readings from the *Resource Book* along with other homework and journal-writing assignments. Across the top of the syllabus is an epigraph selected by Marysa that corresponds to the curriculum's opening identity theme:

> How can you get very far
> If you don't know Who You Are?
> How can you do what you ought
> If you don't know What You've Got?

And if you don't know What To Do
Of all the things in front of you,
Then what you'll have when you are through
Is just a mess without a clue
Of all the best that can come true
If you know What and Which and Who.[5]

The desk arrangement in the classroom maximizes the students' ability to see one another. Two semicircles of eight desks each face each other on the left- and right-hand sides of the room, framed by the meeting/chess area and the row of coat lockers. Marysa's desk—actually a Formica tabletop—sits in the gap between semicircles at the front end of the room. The Ping-Pong table/work area fills in the gap at the other end, thereby completing a disjointed circle. Two short rows of three desks face each other in between the two student arcs. Those who sit here directly face eleven students and have their backs to the remaining eight. The majority of students who sit in the outside semicircles face twenty of the class's twenty-three students. Though all students can see the teacher, no one faces her directly. As students take their seats, I notice that the seating plan is integrated by race, ethnicity, and, to a lesser extent, gender.

"We're going to see a film called *After the First*," Marysa says while rolling the television set to a place where everyone can see it, next to the former Ping-Pong table. "Try to think about what the title might mean as you're watching this." With no further introduction, a student turns off the lights, the remaining students drift back to their seats, and all eyes turn toward the TV.

After the First is a story about a boy's first hunting trip with his father. The outing marks the boy's twelfth birthday. It is in a sense an initiation rite, a "gift" by the boy's father to his son, Steve, which celebrates the son's journey toward manhood by including him in an event shared by generations of men in his family.

Steve's mother is not happy about the outing. Concerned with Steve's safety and seemingly critical of hunting rabbits for sport, she looks on anxiously as her husband and son eagerly leave the house together, nearly identical in their sandy blond hair, khaki hunting jackets, and heavy boots. Her husband makes it clear that each parent has a unique gift to offer. "Nancy," he tells his wife, "that party you gave him last night was very nice, but that was *your* present, not mine. Today is *mine*."

Sitting close together in their pickup truck, father and son share a rapport that is palpable. When the car radio is turned on, we hear a brief news report about the week's casualty figures in Vietnam. Steve is prompted to ask his father if he ever had to kill anyone during the war, but his father's response is vague and almost nonchalant: "Oh, you never really know for sure."

Moments later, the two arrive at their destination. They walk happily through the woods, crunching dead leaves, climbing over fallen trees, crossing brooks and ice patches. Steve soaks in the sights, smells, and sounds of the outdoors, delighting in sharing them with his father. He gets a thorough lesson in how to cock, load, shoot, and carry a gun and clearly enjoys the power he gets from the kick of the rifle.

When Steve's father finally eyes a rabbit, he deftly aims the rifle and fires. Within seconds he has ripped out the animal's organs and pocketed its body. Steve looks on, suddenly horrified and disgusted. Though he has relished hunting in the abstract, he seems to find its reality intolerable. "Don't worry," his father says. "He can't feel anything. He's dead." And then, "It's the life cycle." Steve says, "OK," but it is clear he does not mean it. He hesitates several moments before rejoining his father, mournfully watching a flock of geese as it squawks overhead. As Steve's earlier enthusiasm turns sour, the rapport between father and son begins to dissipate. "What's the matter?" his father asks. "Nothing."

Steve's moment to shoot follows soon after, and it is clear that he is ambivalent about doing so. The camera pans back and forth between Steve's eye and the rabbit's, and from Steve's perspective, we see that his target looks scared: its soft, gray ears are pinned back tight, and its nose is twitching. "Take it! Cock it! Now! Now!

Now!" his father yells excitedly. Steve eventually complies, and the rabbit is blown to pieces.

Though Steve's father ecstatically shouts words of praise, the boy is clearly distressed as he walks mechanically toward his corpse. He asks, "Is two enough?" holding his limp offering at arm's length. His father's empathetic response only serves to underscore the sudden distance between himself and his son: "I know how you feel. I felt that way. Once. Come on. You'll see. After the first time, it gets easier."⁶

As conceived by curriculum designers, the film *After the First* is intended to catalyze classroom discussion about how adolescents can learn to recognize what they believe in and to identify decision-making situations in which they may or may not choose to act on those beliefs. By highlighting differences between Steve's parents and by showing Steve's own internal conflicts in determining what he feels, the film demonstrates that an individual's beliefs necessarily evolve in the context of social relationships and that acting on one's beliefs inevitably affects one's social community. The hunting dilemma presented in the film provokes thinking about violence, aggression, and attitudes toward life (human or otherwise)—issues of central importance later in the semester when students undertake the study of twentieth-century genocide. Placed within the curriculum's opening "Society and the Individual" chapter, however, *After the First* is perhaps most usefully intended to initiate students' exploration of their own personal beliefs about violence, authority, responsibility, and moral choice. By depicting conflicts between different perspectives (both within and between the individuals presented), the film helps bring students' own differences to light.

These differences by and large replicate those portrayed in the film itself: girls tend to side with Steve's mother in decrying the cruelty of hunting, and boys tend to side with his father in claiming hunting to be their natural right. These stereotypical gender responses are not altogether surprising, for as adolescent girls struggle to prove their sensitivity, their male classmates struggle to prove their toughness and manhood. In keeping with dominant societal norms, *After the First* implicitly sanctions these gender responses, while privileging the female response. Highly cognizant of societal expectations of male and female behavior, and, as adolescents, often desirous of approval from their peers, these students can be seen to publicly respond in somewhat expected ways.

After the First is hardly neutral on the ethical dilemma presented to students. The film strikes me as being rather didactic in its criticism of hunting for sport (if not hunting in general), depicting the mother and the hunted rabbit with compassion while portraying the father as brutish and insensitive. The son's moral dilemma over whether or not to shoot is also presented favorably; one is meant to feel for Steve as he suffers under the burden of his father's expectations, and, once he decides to shoot the rabbit, his displeasure in doing so is seen as a moral virtue.

To her credit, Marysa pushes students beyond their relatively facile identification with the simplistic positions portrayed in the film. In keeping with the curriculum's intent (if not with the articulation of that intent as expressed in this particular resource), she urges students to think honestly about how they would act in a situation like the one faced by Steve. She prods them to think about their relations with their own parents and to examine their own decision-making behavior, and provides them with different ways to explore and express their feelings. Her efforts allow for a greater complexity to emerge, for in this classroom exchange, as in others later in the course, a range of student responses unfolds.

Some students take sides quickly and simply, while others are less certain where they stand and are potentially relativistic in their deliberations. Over time, however, one sees that even seemingly rigid stances are softened, and seemingly "relativistic" musings are, in fact, only momentary postures within ongoing attempts to sort out a series of ethical relationships. Interestingly, too, students at times express opinions in their journals that differ from their more public classroom comments. These differences suggest that students are quite conscious of the social arena in which they choose to speak or to remain silent. Like Steve's internal conflict in the resource film, these gaps between students' public and more private personae tell us something important: that individuals form their values in a social context, and that context may make it easier or harder to express and/or act on those values. Here as elsewhere in the course, students are deliberately encouraged to become conscious of the interplay between their personal beliefs and the larger community.

The Classroom

"Take a few minutes to sit quietly and write in your journals," Marysa says once students have finished watching the resource film. She stops the videotape and hits "rewind" while Sandra goes to turn on the lights. "What are your feelings and thoughts about this film?" she asks. The classroom is very quiet while students write, but after a few minutes discussion begins. Students tend to speak directly to each other, at times glancing in Marysa's direction for nods of encouragement or support. Marysa intervenes intermittently to underscore a particular point or to help move the discussion in a certain direction.

> *Marlene:* I don't think Steve's age really had anything to do with it. It's just how he felt about it. He pictured it really different when he was practicing, but he was shocked when he had to kill the rabbit.
>
> *Jess:* My dad hunts a lot. I think it's wrong to kill animals for sport, but it's OK if you need to eat them to live.
>
> *Angela:* I don't think the father should have pushed the boy to follow in his footsteps. He should have asked the boy what he felt. He just didn't want to hurt his father's feelings!
>
> *Amiri:* At first Steve was really excited. But then when he got there, he was really upset.
>
> *Marlene:* I agree with Amiri and Angela. The father didn't talk to him enough and explain things.
>
> *Zeke:* Yeah. The father was trying to make the kid just like him.

Highlighting the curriculum's attention to the importance of parental values in influencing a child's beliefs, Marysa interjects, "Don't parents do that? Do your father or mother teach you like they were taught?"

Susie: It depends. If some parents didn't like the way they were raised, they may raise you exactly the opposite.

Josh: Yeah! My mom is like that. Her mom is really mean, and she's tried to be really nice with me!

Alan: Well, Steve's mother thought he was too young, so his father and mother were different toward him.

Amiri: It seemed to me like the father didn't care about the boy's feelings that much.

Jamal: But Steve wanted to hunt! He just didn't have the stomach for it after he killed.

"Well, what choices did Steve have?" Marysa asks, highlighting Steve's role as a decision maker in the situation presented. Trying to foster students' awareness of their own responsibilities, she presses them to evaluate Steve's behavior in light of his positive feelings for his father and his perception of his father's authority. Students' answers here and later in classroom journals outline three options: resistance, evasion, and acquiescence. Chi-Ho writes, "Steve could have cried out, 'No!' showing that he was not ready and still too young to hunt. He could have missed on purpose. But I think he didn't want to disappoint his father, so he shot." And Jess, grasping the tension between private desire and social consequences: "I think [Steve] had a lot of choices but he thought he had to do what his father wanted. So his choice might have been different if he had been alone." Classroom contributions are in a similar vein:

Yoshi: He could have missed the rabbit on purpose.

Jamal: He could have killed him.

Marlene: He could have said, "No!"

Marysa: Can twelve-year-old kids in every culture say no to their fathers?

Angela: Well, at least he could have said, "I want to shoot at trees."

Marlene: Or he could have just watched his father kill.

Tyrone: But he didn't really realize he was going to kill.

Sandra: Maybe he thought he would kill, but he didn't realize he would end a life.

Jamal: Well, I would kill Thumper!

Marysa rolls her eyes at Jamal—who seems happy to have gotten a rise out of someone—and asks the class, "How did Steve respond to his father's killing the rabbit?" Jamal snickers, "Just like the girls in the room!" and the girls get upset and start to yell.

Though stated provocatively, Jamal's observation is nonetheless astute. Girls and boys do tend to respond differently to the ethical dilemma presented in *After the First*—a difference underscored by the conflict between Steve's mother and father in the resource film. By and large, male students defend hunting on the grounds that it is a fair, just, and even natural act. Noting that animals kill each other to survive in the wild and that violence must therefore be innate, they interpret Steve's hesitancy as a sign of his being "wimpy" rather than as a principled struggle. As such, most boys fail to see Steve's dilemma as a moral conflict, whether over the ethics of hunting or over whether to follow or disobey his father's desires. Disparaging Steve's squeamishness by likening him to girls in the classroom, Jamal and his peers distance themselves from their female classmates and from their different way of interpreting the situation portrayed.

Girls, by contrast, tend to sympathize with Steve's difficult choice. Decrying the "cruelty" of hunting for sport and expressing concern for the welfare of the rabbit, they muse over the comparative value of human versus animal life and seem, at points, almost alarmingly relativistic. Their comments not only identify Steve's moral conflict but suggest that they themselves are wrestling with the same moral dilemmas.

"Do you remember what the father said to Steve?" Marysa asks. "He said, 'It's the life cycle.'"

> *Angela:* But it's not! It's other animals who kill each other. Not humans with a shotgun!
> *Jamal:* Animals kill each other, same as humans.
> *Josh:* If a rabbit had a gun it would use it to kill a human!
> *Sandra:* Is an animal's life worth less than a human life?

Sandra's question is provocative. Several students shout out answers simultaneously, and it soon becomes difficult to hear what anyone has to say. Marysa lets the enthusiasm grow for a moment and then channels it by calling for a vote. She asks, "How many here believe an animal's life is worth less than a human's?" Seven boys raise their hands while the girls look on disapprovingly. "And how many believe their lives are equal?" Six female hands are raised. I realize that about eight students, most of them boys, have abstained from voting. Some look bored and distracted, while others seem engaged but hesitant to take a stand. Tyrone expands the discussion beyond the frame of the purely personal: "Well, society thinks an animal's life is worth less. I mean, they don't announce on TV that a rabbit has died."

> *Mandy:* It's just like that video game, "Oregon Trail," that the boys play all the time. It teaches you to kill things.
> *Josh:* Man, that's a great game! And it's crazy not to kill rabbits, say, to test for cancer.
> *Angela:* If you had to kill either your mom or your cat, it'd be hard.

I am somewhat startled by Angela's self-imposed dilemma, but no one else seems to hear it, or if so, to mind. Mandy's comment, too, seems to come a little out of left field, but Marysa reins it in by widening the lens a bit. "What about violence? Is it a natural thing or—" "Yeah!" interrupts Josh, and Sara shoots him a look like he's crazy—"is it taught?" Marysa finishes.

Alan: It can be taught, but it's also in you.

Jess: I think that's right. You're born with a certain amount of it, but you can be taught to use it or not.

Angela: I think you're born with it a little, because if a two-year-old has a toy and another kid takes it away, they'll hit them!

Sandra pulls the discussion back to the concrete: "Even so, it's slaughter if you don't eat the animal!" Marysa explains even-handedly, "Lots of people in the NRA are defending having rifles and hunting as a sport. Others are saying it's OK to hunt, but only if you're eating it. Still others are saying that hunting is a constitutionally protected right." Josh, son of an attorney who works for the ACLU, answers matter-of-factly, "It *is* protected."

Angela is still caught up in her hypothetical choice between mother and cat. Landing where she can with certainty, she comments: "Vegetables are lower than animals, I think." Various students follow Andrea's lead by offering their own thoughts on the interrelationship of human, plant, and animal life. Their contributions seem only loosely connected to one another.

Abby: But you know, some scientists have proven that plants scream when they're torn.

Jess: Well, killing the rain forests in Latin America is like killing off a race or something. It will have a domino effect on everything else.

Sandra: Then you'll have to determine what's superior and what's inferior.

Duane: I was watching a program on Channel 2, and it said whales don't eat humans.

Jess: Yeah, they're vegetarians.

Josh: Well, walking down a street, you can't walk without stepping on an ant.

Marysa: But is there a distinction to be made, Josh, between that and kids who intentionally try to squash them?

Angela: Humans are the only animals who kill just to kill.
Josh: That's 'cause they're the only ones smart enough!

Listening to the students in this classroom, I realize that boys and girls seem to clash not because they speak from opposite ends of the same argument (for example, no girls contend that it is unnatural for animals to kill each other and no boys contend that killing for sport is not cruel), but because they construct the argument itself differently. In this instance, girls tend to focus on emotional issues of attachment and caring when addressing the hunting dilemma, while boys focus, instead, on intellectual issues of rights and reciprocity.

These distinct positions are in keeping with the different moral perspectives noted by Carol Gilligan and her colleagues. They have identified two distinct moral "voices" within individuals: a "care voice," which highlights issues of relationships, and a "justice voice," which highlights issues of fairness and equality.[7] Those speaking with a "care voice" tend to focus on issues of attachment and connectedness when reckoning with moral conflicts. Seeing moral value in attending to the connections among individuals, they render problematic instances in which connection is severed or strained—through inattentiveness, a lack of responsiveness, and so forth. Moral behavior is understood as that which furthers caring, connected relationships, and a moral problem as that which endangers these connections.

Individuals speaking with a "justice voice" are similarly concerned with moral issues but attend to different elements in any given situation. In evaluating a moral dilemma, these individuals tend to focus on issues of rights, equality, and fairness. Moral behavior is construed as that which adheres to just principles or standards, and a moral problem as that which violates these principles through depriving any party of their just due.

Given these different orientations, it is not surprising that individuals may in fact differ over whether they even recognize a moral conflict to exist in a given situation. Evaluation of the problem presented and how it should be resolved in part depends on who is viewing the situation and on which ethic (justice or care) is perceived to be violated. While Gilligan and her colleagues argue that both boys and girls possess the capacity for both moral orientations, they find that the "care voice" usually predominates in girls and the "justice voice" in boys. These cleavages appear to be borne out in the classroom exchange described.

In this instance, Jamal and Josh can be seen to speak in a "justice voice" when they focus on neither the value of the rabbit's life nor their own feelings in relation to it, but instead on the individual's intrinsic right to hunt. So, too, do they defend Steve's father's actions on the grounds of an assumed reciprocity between animals and humans; they do not by and large comment on his treatment of his son. Jamal argues that "animals kill each other, same as humans," and Josh insists that "if a rabbit had a gun, it would use it to kill a human." Seeing animals and human beings as similarly positioned, neither Jamal nor Josh considers hunting to be oppressive. Finding that no moral principles are violated in this case, neither construes hunting as a moral problem.

Abby, Angela, Sandra, Marlene, and Jess construct the moral question at issue in hunting quite differently. These girls focus on the feelings of both the rabbit and Steve and condemn Steve's father, furthermore, for being insensitive toward his son. Their classroom comments and journal contributions underscore the interconnectedness of human beings, animals, and nature. Since "hunting for sport" severs connections between living creatures, they consider it "insensitive" and "cruel"; since Steve loves his father and clearly wants to please him, they consider his father's "pressuring" insensitive. Sandra writes in her journal with conviction, at times capitalizing words for greater emphasis: "I thought the movie was insensitive by showing the dead bunny. Death should never be taken lightly no matter if it is a bunny or a living human being. You should NEVER FEEL COMFORTABLE KILLING anything if it's your 1st time or your 100th time." And Abby: "Hunting is a senseless and cruel sport. And I guess that is what bothers me most about it (it is a sport). Steve finds out after shooting an animal for the first time how senseless it is. The father, because he had done it before, found it easier. But it would never get easier for me." In this context, Steve's conflict is indeed a moral one.

Girls' particular attentiveness to issues of relationship can be seen in another curricular example from this chapter. In the identity chart exercise described earlier, boys and girls tended to include different kinds of subject matter on their personal ID charts. Generally speaking, girls listed relationships with others as an essential component of their identity, while boys nearly always failed to do so. Of the nine girls who completed this assignment, every last one included mothers, fathers, and siblings on their chart. By contrast, only three out of the nine boys who made ID charts mentioned family members at all, and those who did so included them differently than girls.

Boys who addressed family in fact catalogued family members, listing them by their proper names as if to suggest their existence as autonomous individuals. Hee Joon wrote: mother–Mrs. Sook Joe Lee, sister–Wong Joon Lee, and brother–Bok Joon Lee. By contrast, girls described the quality of their relationships with family members, describing when these relations were supportive and loving as well as when they were estranged or removed. Abby labeled separate rays of her chart "loving family," "close to parents," "youngest of three siblings," and "loved." Marlene simply noted that she has "very supportive parents." Other girls recorded painful breaks in relationships. Susie wrote: "Parents divorced," "live with my mom," "family lives in Ohio." And Alison: "small immediate family," "parents divorced," "live in Cambridge with mom," "and Boston with dad." No girls recorded the proper names of family members on these charts.

By noting these differences, I do not mean to suggest that girls care more about familial relationships than boys do, or, harking back to the hunting dilemma, that girls care about animals while boys are indifferent to them. As Gilligan and many other feminist theorists have suggested, articulated gender differences such as these are the product of social and cultural norms rather than biological determinants. The cultural histories of boys and girls in this classroom emerge against the backdrop of a society that, even today, emphasizes caretaking roles for women and girls and independence for boys and men. Though these social values are becoming more multifaceted, what constitutes "strength" in this culture is still to a considerable extent seen differently by gender: for boys, strength may mean physical endurance, courage, and lack of emotion; for girls, it means sensitivity, caring, and emotional depth. Adolescent boys and girls are well aware of dominant gender roles; given the enormous importance of peer acceptance among this age population, it is not surprising that the opinions they voiced publicly in the classroom—and those they at times expressed in more private journals—by and large conform to socially sanctioned prescriptions for gender.

But Marysa's homework assignment pushes students to rethink the sometimes pat positions they have argued in class. Following the curriculum's intent to have students critically explore their own values in light of the social context through which they emerge, she asks students to answer three questions: "How does Steve change during the movie?" "How do his parents contribute to that change?" "What were Steve's choices?" In responding, some boys privately voice feelings that contradict (or at least complicate) the dominant "male" position they have argued earlier.

Josh is the most notable case in point. While in public he champions one's "right" to hunt and defends his own enjoyment of a video game, his private ruminations suggest some critique of both realms: "It's interesting how in the U.S. guns are shown as something besides what they are, tools for killing. T.V. plays a big part of that image guns have." Perhaps less dramatically, two other boys who had remained silent in class express qualified opposition to hunting in their journals. Zeke writes, "I can't believe that Steve shot the rabbit, because he doesn't seem like that kind of person. Personally I could never kill an animal unless I was starving to death because I find it sick." And Yoshi: "I think hunting for sport or fun is wrong, but if it was needed it is all right because it is the life cycle."

These gaps between boys' public personae (whether expressed through boisterous commentary or passive silence) and their more private reflections say something about the performative character of discourse: people say different things in different contexts. Aware of cultural constraints against seeming too sensitive or too emotional, and no doubt concerned with winning the approval of their peers, these young males publicly articulate (or at least refrain from contradicting) a culturally sanctioned, gender-appropriate voice.

To my mind, this does not suggest that the opinions students articulated in class were insincere, but rather that they may have been partial. As the opening lesson itself demonstrates through young Steve's internal quandary, individual beliefs are complex and multifaceted, at times in flux, and usually inextricably tied to a social community.

By encouraging students publicly and privately to explore their views, Marysa and the FHAO curriculum seek to engender complex thinking within and among members of the class. This pedagogical goal is mirrored by conflicts depicted in the curricular lesson itself: Steve's internal struggles dramatize students' own questions and confusions. *Resource Book* questions about Steve's changes in perspective ("What is Steve's mood as the film begins? As it ends? At what point does his attitude begin to change, and why? How would you describe Steve as a person?"[8]) suggest that conflict may be an inevitable part of defining one's values and beliefs. Still other homework questions ("How do [Steve's] parents contribute to that change? What were Steve's choices?") situate individual struggles within one's relationships and social responsibilities. By raising the subject of parental authority and by highlighting Steve's choices in relation to his father, this curricular lesson projects Steve—and, by extension, this classroom of students—into the role of decision maker. Joining Steve's dilemma with the public and private reflections of these same students, this lesson intends to show that making a responsible decision requires, first, knowing where one stands, and second, reckoning with its consequences.

Though I find much to commend in this opening exercise, opponents of moral education programs might find much to criticize. The fact that Facing History's resource film is didactic, for example, might be taken as proof that students are being indoctrinated with a liberal agenda. The fact that Steve's moral dilemma resulted from a conflict he had with his father might be interpreted as a challenge to parental authority, another of the critics' concerns. Opponents might also fault Facing History for showing a young boy engaged in a moral conflict in the first place, since some contend that adolescents are unprepared and ill-equipped to deal with painful moral dilemmas.

But building on curricular intent as well as sound teaching experience, Marysa's classroom practice actually goes beyond the confines of the particular resource film she used in class. Her questions prod students to explore their differences and to examine conflicting values they may have within themselves. Students are responsive to Marysa's critical questioning and thus perhaps hesitant to wholly accept the implicit message of the resource film. Like their peers who attended the Massachusetts Civil Liberties Union's Rap About Racism, they come into the classroom already conscious of some of their own convictions about right and wrong. With their teacher's guidance, they engage in a debate that helps them think and rethink their convictions in light of the opposing viewpoints they heard. Students are neither completely passive nor completely impenetrable regarding the diverse perspectives voiced in class. They sift and sort through conflicting views, clarifying their own thoughts along the way.

The debate students engaged in was lively, and most seemed interested and involved during class. Though talk was at times contentious, the class remained a community throughout. This reflects the skill with which Marysa had worked to create a classroom environment of respect and trust. That environment was also nurtured by the school's commitment to diversity, and by its concerted effort (conveyed both programmatically and symbolically) to have students see difference as a strength rather than a weakness. Facing History's own efforts to engender personal, critical reflection no doubt contributed to this effort, as did the strengths and capacities of students themselves—their desire to sort out where they stand and their ripeness for engaging in just such debates. This ripeness is, of course, vital to students' learning.

This opening lesson certainly raises questions worthy of debate. But it also shows the power of a teacher, curriculum, school, and community working together, reinforcing each others' efforts to achieve common goals.

Chapter Three

"We Don't Believe
Everything that We Hear"

"I need to review the ground rules for the Facing History unit," Marysa begins one damp morning in March. "First, there will be no putdowns of other people. Even if people say things you disagree with, you need to give them your respect. Second, I want you to try to avoid making judgments about other people's ideas and beliefs. Third, we're going to have several guests come into our class during the next ten weeks." "Survivors?" Sandra interrupts. "Yes, sometimes survivors, but other people, too. And when they're here there will be no leaving the room, no walking around, and no sharpening pencils. I want you to be respectful to these guests."

Several weeks into the Facing History course, today's lesson is one in a series concerning questions of religious difference and discrimination. Drawing from the third chapter of the Facing History *Resource Book*, "Antisemitism: A Case Study of Prejudice and Discrimination," these classes explore the historical roots of antisemitism, its contemporary resonances, and the causes and consequences of conflicts arising over differences in religious belief. More broadly conceived, these classes introduce students to the notion of multiple perspectives or "truths." Through using a series of fictional and historical readings as a springboard for classroom discussion, the classes provoke students to critically reflect on their own cultural beliefs in light of the beliefs of others. In this instance as in others later on, the curriculum does not intend to suggest that all perspectives and beliefs are equally valid—Marysa's opening comment about "not judging others" notwithstanding. Instead, the program seeks to help students recognize that their beliefs are, in part, culturally determined; to understand that these beliefs are often linked to power relations within any given society; and to examine their beliefs and attitudes about "others" in light of this critical understanding. "In this chapter we present antisemitism as a case study in discrimination," the *Resource Book* explains:

> Initially, we investigate the phenomenon of antisemitism as it relates to all kinds of hatred, especially those familiar to our students, anti-black, anti-white, anti-Irish, anti-other. In the initial chapters of this curriculum we explored ways an individual maintains his or her identity. And in this chapter we learn that groups, too, try to maintain their identities. One way a group or society develops its identity is to distinguish itself from other groups, through the characteristics that distinguish it from other groups, or through the ideas and ideals it advocates. If a group or society likes what it stands for, then what it stands for is "good," and what it is *not* can be construed as "bad." This way of thinking inevitably leads to prejudice, whether it is adopted by an individual or a society.[1]

All week, students have been exploring this lesson by reading a fictional story set in the sixteenth century about a young Christian boy filled with antisemitic prejudices. Written by Sulamith Ish-Kishor, *The Boy of Old Prague* focuses on Thomas, the serf of an abusive lord, who is sold to a wealthy Jew in Prague's Jewish ghetto. Thomas approaches his new life with trepidation, full of fears based on Christian superstitions. However, once inside the ghetto gates, he gets an entirely different picture of Jewish life: here he finds love, fairness, decency, and a new master who treats him far better than his original lord had done. Newly critical of Christianity's misguided beliefs about Jews, Thomas becomes increasingly torn between the values of his original (yet ignorant) community and his own first-hand knowledge and experience.

Through Thomas's transformation, students learn of differences *between* coexisting yet conflicting religious cultures during the sixteenth century and also *within* members of the same religious community. (Thomas becomes critical of the dominant Christian position on Jews, yet he remains a devout Christian throughout the book.) Thomas notes at one point that "a certain writer . . . had been declaring that the Talmud . . . ordered Jews to kill Christian children and to drink their blood at the Passover. . . . I know that once I had believed all this myself, but I could have told [people] now it was not true. . . . But people did not seem to care about these things; my own family . . . listened doubtfully to what I told them about the truth of these matters."[2] When a pogrom destroys the Jewish ghetto later on in the book, Thomas is filled with shame and remorse. He concludes with the hope that one day "we shall learn that the God of mercy is the same God, no matter where we find Him."[3]

Marysa and select students take turns reading this story out loud during afternoon reading class. The remaining students listen quietly, legs sprawled and heads resting on their desks. Several appear tired and quite a few seem bored. Whatever their level of interest, most have easily grasped the story's central message. Asked by Marysa to comment on what factors changed Thomas's thinking, for example, Amiri writes in his journal: "When Thomas worked for the lord he was your average racist ignorant Christian boy. He would think and say stupid things like Jews killed Christian boys and drank their blood. When Thomas was placed as a servant for a Jew he practically wanted to kill himself because of all of the stupid things put in his head about Jews. After a while living with the Jews Thomas understood them a lot more. He saw they weren't bad at all, and really were nice and caring people. Finally he realized how ridiculous those prejudices everyone had against the Jews were."

In subsequent lessons, students continue to explore differing perspectives on a variety of issues: in a reading on the Treaty of Versailles, students examine postwar policy options from the vantage point of both victors and losers; in a related class on the postwar redrawing of the map of Europe, a familiar Eurocentric map is displayed alongside one from a Southern Hemisphere perspective.

"That map's upside down!" students initially exclaim on seeing the latter map. "No, it's done from the perspective of Australia," one boy corrects after studying it more closely.

"What have we been talking about all week?" Marysa asks this morning after laying down Facing History's ground rules for respect. "Prejudice and intolerance," answers Tyrone. "Human behavior?" queries Angela. Alison adds, "Antisemitism and discrimination."

It is 9:00 A.M. Students slump comfortably in their chairs. Some focus on Marysa, while others are still struggling to wake up. Separated by a distance of several feet, Josh silently but obviously mouths something to Zeke that Zeke cannot understand. Marysa ignores this interaction, and Josh eventually gives up.

"What does *antisemitism* mean?" Marysa asks. This is one of the week's new vocabulary words, so students refer to their notes and read different dictionary definitions out loud: "Hostility towards Jews." "Hatred and prejudice against Jews." "Dislike and fear of Jews and Jewish things." There is a brief discussion about these definitions, and occasionally *The Boy of Old Prague* is brought in as an example. Then, departing from this fictionalized account, Marysa probes students' own beliefs about Jews.

Marysa: How can you tell if someone is Jewish?

Josh: (Describing himself) By their looks. Jews *look* different. They have dark hair and dark eyes, and they wear glasses.

Alison: Can't you tell by their last names?

Marysa: Sometimes, but not all the time. You can't always tell by their looks or their last names.

Angela: You can tell by their different beliefs and rituals.

Jess: Their life-styles are sometimes different.

Hee Joon: Maybe they have different cultures and celebrate different traditions and things.

Marysa: Hee Joon brings up a good point. When some people came to this country, they tried to assimilate, to blend in. If people want to be part of a new culture, they may want to blend in, not to be a "them," but to be an "us." But histori-

cally, Jews have not wanted to assimilate, to give up their
own culture.

Nora: People try to adjust but also to keep their background.
That's how it is with my family and Mexico.

Josh, the only Jewish student in the class, authoritatively disagrees.
"It all depends. There are different branches of Jews—Orthodox,
Conservative, and Reform—and some try to adjust, but others
don't. So you can't really say."

A thirteen-year-old boy preparing for his Bar Mitzvah this
semester, Josh defines himself as "culturally, not religiously, Jewish."
He sits at the end of one arched row of desks in class, just next to
me at the Ping-Pong table, and nods to me—the only other Jewish
person in the classroom—at salient points throughout the course.
For example, when a young Jewish boy in *The Boy of Old Prague*
gets Bar Mitzvahed, Josh signals proudly that he is next. When
Marysa asks students to define the word *kosher* in the context of this
same reading, Josh jumps in to supply the answer (and then brags
loudly, "Melinda, aren't I right?").

Josh seems slightly more interested in *The Boy of Old Prague*
than many of his classmates, perhaps because he feels more
personally connected to it. In a later interview, Josh remarks that
his own identification as a Jew—and his singular religious status
among his classmates—deeply affects his experience of the Facing
History course:

> It's *hard* to be the only person in the group that this is like person-
> ally affecting to . . . 'cause we studied the slave trade two years ago,
> and I'm sure it was hard for black people or whatever, but they're
> almost 50 percent of the class or more. And, if you're all *alone* and
> you're learning about something, it's a lot harder. You see everyone
> else like listening, but not like, *feeling it*. 'Cause you don't really *feel*
> something unless it's your own people. That's true. You can't really
> feel problems that black people go through. You can understand it,
> but you can't feel it.

In fact, Josh's perception of his class is somewhat distorted: blacks comprise only a quarter of the class's makeup, whites comprise nearly 50 percent, and Hispanics and Asians constitute the remainder. Josh's feelings of isolation may account for his misperception of the student body: conscious that he is "all alone" as a Jew, he sees others as stronger and more united than they perhaps are.

For the next several minutes of class, students discuss the tension between assimilation and retaining one's cultural identity. Some non-Jews share Josh's belief that "Jews look different." When I mention that I—a light-brown-haired, green-eyed, light-skinned woman—am Jewish, many express surprise. Eventually the conversation moves toward a faith more familiar to most of the class, and Andrea and Duane, two strongly identified Christian students, speak up.

Marysa: Who was Christ?
Duane: (Matter-of-factly) The son of God.
Marysa: Does everyone here believe that?
Duane: No.
Marysa: What was Mary's religion?
Duane: (After a long pause, and softly) Jewish.
Angela: Jesus *was* Jewish but then after he died he became
    Christian.

Marysa asks for a show of hands: How many in the room are Catholic? Five. How many are Protestant? Also five. How many are Jewish? Josh's hand shoots up proudly, and I also raise mine. Marysa, born and raised a Catholic, cautiously lifts her arm up halfway and explains, "I'm in transition. I'm thinking of going and living as a citizen in Israel, and if I do that I must be Jewish"—though in fact it is possible, if difficult, to acquire Israeli citizenship without being Jewish.

A series of disjointed questions follow in which students voice some very basic questions about religious belief. Some are confused by the difference between Catholicism and Protestantism. Sandra asks, "Do all Catholics and Protestants believe that Jesus was Christ?" Jamal speculates, "Don't they both believe in the same book?" Another wonders, "Are Protestants and Catholics both Christians, or are Christians a different thing?"

Marysa attempts to clarify religious similarities and differences by returning to history: "Have any of you ever heard of Martin Luther?" "Yeah, *King*!" Jamal answers. "No, before him," Marysa corrects. "He's the man King was named after." She goes on to explain why Luther broke away from the Catholic Church, how Protestantism developed, and how it is that both Catholics and Protestants are part of the Christian faith.

Abby has become impatient with this discussion. Irreverent and perhaps intentionally provocative, she interjects: "You know about Mary? I've been thinking about this a lot: I think Joseph got Mary pregnant, but she wasn't married so to hide their sin they said God did it!" Abby is a self-proclaimed unbeliever. In her classroom journal, she labels one ray of her personal identity chart "atheist" alongside others labeled "determined," "athlete," "supportive," and "have a loving family."

Marysa seems a bit bothered by Abby's remark. She mutters something sardonically under her breath and tries to move on quickly. She asks her students, "What's a miracle?" with serious intent, but their answers are probably not what she had hoped for.

Abby: (Undaunted) *Not* getting Mary pregnant!
Sandra: Finding a parking space in a crowded mall!
Zeke: People coming back from the dead.
Sandra: Ohhh! Let's see *Pet Sematary*!

Students respond enthusiastically to Sandra's suggestion and the class soon becomes a cacophony of excited "Yeah! Yeah!," laughter, and jokes. Sandra and Zeke animatedly review the plot line of *Pet Sematary* and delight in recalling its most gruesome parts. Jamal asks Marysa about freezing people and bringing them back to life.

When things eventually quiet down, students venture their

own understandings of faith. Religious feelings vary widely, and students seem comfortable with hearing a variety of opinions expressed. Duane and Angela's religious conviction runs deep; Abby's atheism appears equally inviolable; Josh defines himself as a cultural Jew; Sandra and Daphine are openly questioning. Marysa allows these different perspectives to emerge, facilitating exchange by a variety of means: prodding students directly ("Does everyone here believe that?"), letting students challenge each other, and challenging the students herself to help them define their own beliefs and feelings.

Duane, a Jehovah's Witness, is affable with his classmates but sets himself apart in countless daily ways. In keeping with his religion's dictate to refrain from public celebration and ceremony, he leaves the room whenever class birthdays or other special events are celebrated. "I don't even take one bite of cake," he tells me.

> The only group I've ever been a part of is Jehovah's Witness, and I'm proud of it. We don't do a lot of the things that other religions and other people do in the world. There's no sex before marriage. We don't salute flags or praise rulers of the earth, like they were a God. We don't smoke. We don't use bad language. And we stay away from things that aren't clean. We don't hurt anybody, we don't use weapons. You know, we try to be no part of this world, just as Jesus Christ was, when he was on the earth.

Duane's immediate, unequivocal response to Marysa's question, "Who was Christ?" ("The son of God"), his more hesitant acknowledgment that not everyone regards him as such, and his admission that Jesus was Jewish, must be understood in light of his deeply held religious faith. Given Duane's strong convictions, I wondered how he felt about the range of religious beliefs openly expressed in class. His comments in our interview suggest an unshaken certainty in the "rightness" of his faith, a somewhat partial understanding of history (which ironically sidesteps certain class lectures and readings), and a solid, though qualified, respect for the beliefs of others:

I feel Jehovah's Witness is the true religion. Back in the first century, that was the main religion. Christian it was called, back in Jerusalem, everybody in that city was a Christian, and they followed, they obeyed, they read the Bible, and they praised one God, and that's the way it was. But as men spread out around the world, men had different beliefs, and also, the spirit force, Satan, switched them to other different religions. . . . When we go door to door trying to talk to others we don't try to change their thoughts, but we see what they think are differences, and if they feel what we're saying is right, they can have a free home bible study, and somebody will even come and speak to them. . . . I feel that this is the true religion and everybody should be following it. But, then again, there's other religions in the world and people feel like that's the right religion, so they may do so.

Angela shares Duane's Christian convictions, though she is not a Jehovah's Witness. A soft-spoken yet vocal girl, she wears a crucifix to class each day and labels one ray of her identity chart "religious." Her faith is evident in her classroom contributions. In subsequent classes she speaks knowledgeably about the Gospels and, at a later point, interprets contemporary political claims to the land of Israel in light of the Hebrew Bible. Angela's friends also recognize that religion is a defining feature of her life. "We all have our different things," Jess told me one afternoon by way of explaining which elements she considered important to her own identity. "Like, Abby and Sandra, they swim. Alison plays the flute and she takes ballet. And Angela, she plays the viola and she's very, very religious. She goes to church a lot, and orchestra."

Other classmates are less clear about questions of faith. Inspired by the *Pet Sematary* discussion, Daphine writes in her journal after class, "Marysa, I would like to know if you could ask the class as a class activity to go on with this conversation about what they think will happen to them when their time to die comes." Marysa responds sensitively, prodding Daphine to define her own assumptions but also to share them with her classmates: "Daphine, please talk to me about this. I'd love to have this class discussion. What do you think happens?" Daphine writes back: "Well, I'm Baptist and I believe if you do your duty as a Christian should that you will go to heaven. But if you kill and such sins like that you will go to the place down under which is hell."

Still other students confront each other more directly.

Jess: Why does everyone assume God is a man. Why couldn't it be a female?

Melody: (Self-evidently) Because he got Mary pregnant! And since Jesus Christ is white, they also know God is white!

Jess: That wouldn't be true, given where he was born.

Mandy: I saw this Indiana Jones movie, and this guy was searching for the Holy Grail. He had to do all these faith things, and he had to take a leap of faith to prove what he believed was true.

Josh: I could be wrong, but I think that with the stories in any religion's bible, it's not that they're true or false, it's the *values* behind them that matter.

It is worth remembering that these personal reflections were in fact instigated by a somewhat removed intellectual exercise—students' engagement with a fictional text set in the 1500s. Though *The Boy of Old Prague* appeared less than riveting for most students, it clearly served them well as a jumping-off point for a more contemporary and personal exchange. Marysa builds on this personal engagement in subsequent class assignments. "We're going to be talking about religious differences for the next several weeks, and, as we do, I want you to think about your own experiences of labeling and prejudice. In your journals, try to answer the following questions: What prejudices do my friends, family, neighborhood, and region of the country have? What prejudices do *I* have? What are the causes of prejudice?"

In answer to the first question, Susie writes in her journal: "My friends have prejudices against 'nerds' (smart people are nerds) and 'geeks' (people who aren't caught up with the styles). My mother has prejudices against 'boys who will break your heart.' My relatives have prejudices about Blacks (they steal), Chinese (they're weird), and any minority group." Though no students take direct responsibility for their own prejudicial attitudes, Yoshi's answer to Marysa's second question comes the closest to being self-critical: "I think people tend not to see their own prejudices so they think they don't have prejudices but from other people's view they do. I might have one but maybe I myself don't see it or notice it."

Students' understandings of what causes prejudice are diverse; some attribute it to personal experience, while others point to more systemic, cultural, or politically based reasons. Examples of these different understandings include:

> *Abby*: I think two of the main things which cause prejudice are ignorance and the lack of an open mind.
>
> *Jess*: I think some causes of prejudice are fear of what is unknown or different. Maybe if you have a bad experience with one person you might think that everyone else like them is the same way they are. Or maybe they don't like the way they are and therefore they feel they have to find someone worse than themselves.
>
> *Hee Joon*: Maybe some people don't like other cultural groups living in their areas. Some cultural groups might not get along well with people from another cultural group. Two or more different groups' ancestors might have been enemies. Or there might have been some racial or political or religious happening in which the victim's close friends or relatives or cultural group offended the victimizer, who is in a different race or religion or political group.

Tables and Chairs

Two days later, students greet their first "guest" of the Facing History and Ourselves course. Steve Cohen, a former teacher and principal at a private high school outside of Boston, is now a member of the FHAO staff. A wiry, balding white man with thick black glasses, he is anything but imposing; he is wearing baggy gray pants and white tennis shoes, and his green work shirt is not tucked in. He is energetic, witty, and immediately electrifying.

The twenty-three students of Marysa's class are crowded together with twenty-odd other students from Betty Lou's class next door. Betty Lou is a veteran teacher of FHAO and the only other teacher of the combined seventh and eighth grades in the Evers school's Open Program. Throughout the school year, she and Marysa coordinate teaching strategy and lesson plans. During the FHAO course, these two loosely defined "team teachers" meet regularly to discuss how the course is going and to schedule shared resources and guest speakers. Their respective students pass in and out of each others' rooms throughout the day, playing Ping-Pong together and exchanging homework notes and candy. This morning, each group of students seems happy to be with its friends from next door.

"How do you define religion?" Steve Cohen begins. "It's a person's beliefs," answers a student of Betty Lou's.

Steve: I believe in that table. Is that religion?

Josh: Could be!

Steve: How so?

Josh: If you use the table as a symbol, and you make up all sorts of little stories about it, morals and things like that, then it could be your religion.

Steve: Wow! What's your name?

Josh: Josh.

Steve: Well done, Josh! That's pretty good! Religion comes from the Latin word *religio*. And *legio*, in Latin (he writes each word on the chalkboard) means "ligament." Religion literally means that which binds us together!

Abe: People need a way to explain things they don't understand.

Steve: OK, Abe, that's a good point! How people come to understand their world is very important. And someone once said—this is a famous quote—that if you don't *believe,* you can't really *understand.*

Walking briskly around the crowded room, Steve puts different religious beliefs in historical perspective. First he explains that the ancient Romans believed in many gods; he then notes that Jews, Christians, and Moslems believe in only one god, and atheists, he concludes, do not believe in any.

Students assiduously copy Steve's chalkboard scrawl into their journals. Sandra writes: "Polytheism: Believing in more than one god. Monotheism: Believing in just one god: Judaism, Christianity, Islam. Atheism: Don't believe in any god." Steve continues: "Religion was key to the Romans. And one place they conquered they came across a people who believed in *one* God, not many. When polytheism meets the idea of monotheism—ouch!"

"But how can one belief conquer another belief?" Jamal asks, and Jess answers him, "By pressuring the other people to conform to their ways, like in *The Boy of Old Prague.* The lord pressured Jews to change to Christianity, and when they didn't, he burnt down the ghetto." Jamal does not buy it: "One belief may win out, but it's not necessarily better than another belief."

With spontaneity and humor, Steve suggests a quick role play to explore the dynamic raised by Jamal and Jess. Picking up on Josh's earlier remark, Steve divides the class in half: some students become followers of "the religion of Tables," while others are of the "Chair" persuasion. An animated debate ensues in which the newer, monotheistic Chairs fight with the Tables to practice their religious beliefs. Students defend their arbitrary identities with zealousness and passion, relishing the animated exchange. As Steve races around the room, students toss out various means by which the minority Chairs may be subordinated by their longer-established, polytheistic rulers. Their ideas (restrictive laws, military battles, slavery, torture) combine tactics from *The Boy of Old Prague* with those of *Rambo.*

Alan: But it's crazy! What happens if it's all one big lie, and then they've killed millions and millions of people for nothing!

Melody: Why don't they just stop if they realize they're not really getting anywhere?

Steve: You're raising some very real psychological questions about what people believe in, why they do, and what they do about it! I suspect that through this course you're going to look again and again at the things you believe in and ask yourself, "Why *do* I believe in that?"

Returning to history, Steve describes how the monotheistic Jews were conquered by the Babylonians in 586 B.C. Their Temple destroyed and their homes ruined, Jews were driven from their "holy land." While living in the "Diaspora," Jewish scholars kept their faith alive by writing down the customs and practices of their people. Thus when Babylonia was conquered and the Jews returned to their homeland some 150 years later, the "Hebrew Bible" helped this new generation practice the faith of its ancestors.

Several students seem troubled by the notion of multiple religious perspectives. Discomfited by the idea that no faith is "truer" than the next, these students have a hard time granting each truth its legitimacy. Craving the absolute, they transpose their uncertainty onto an either-or framework: if multiple truths can be said to coexist, then any single claim is somehow illegitimate—a "lie."

Jamal: But I don't get something. If I tell a lie to Alan and he believes it, and he tells Bok Joon and Josh and they believe it, and it spins around and around, and it comes back in a month, then maybe it's the same story and maybe not, but it could all be based on a lie!

Nata: And if it's all lies that fit together like a puzzle, then no one tries to say it's not true. Like, no one says, Jesus couldn't have been there, or something like that.

Steve: Well, over the years, many, many people have read the

Hebrew Bible and the New Testament and done archeological digs and other things to try to find evidence to show that Jesus was there. So what we're really saying is not that religion is a lie . . .

Nata: It's exaggerated.

Steve: Well, some stories may be exaggerated, but the more important point is simply that people believe these things to be true. And remember this: what is true in history is not nearly as important as what people believe is true. . . . Faith is going to be very important to think about in this course. We're not going to tell you this faith is right and this faith is wrong. Nobody can argue that *your* belief in God is any better or worse than anyone else's belief in God. That's something to think about.

It is almost noon. For the next thirty minutes, students get a whirlwind tour through the teachings of Jesus and the "Jewish Christians"; clashes between Jesus and the Romans; the rise of Christianity; and the Gospels of the Christian Bible. This intellectual tour is backed up by readings in the FHAO text that attempt to place the origins of Christianity in historical perspective and in a critical context:

The followers of Jesus, viewed by the Romans as just another troublesome challenge to authority, began to form their new identity as Christians. Distinctions between Jews and Christians were defined during Roman times as new "groups" became different from "others." As new groups looked for converts, certain laws and traditions came under re-interpretation and became known as "old" in contrast to the "new" (old testament, new testament), and in time some negative connotations were institutionalized. For those who were interested in identifying a new group as the enemy, there are writings of critical figures in Christian history that can be seen as "energizing factors which contribute to the pumping up of modern antisemitism." Some scholars look to the writings of Matthew and

John, for example, as telling the story of the crucifixion of Jesus in different times to different audiences. . . .

As one explores the historical roots of antisemitism, it is important to recognize that what some historians, scholars, and people of faith consider historical documents, others consider to be indisputable words of God and therefore not open to analysis and interpretation. Most textbooks avoid bringing up these delicate subjects because it is so easy to offend one faith or another. Our attempt is to expose intolerance when it is directed at others. If certain documents and writings of innocent intent have been abused and used to hurt others, then there is merit in thinking about how this happened.[4]

Class is over. Tables and Chairs file out of the classroom and head for the cafeteria as noisily as possible. For the students of Marysa's class, tonight's homework is to "interview someone about a religion different from yours." Though well intentioned, this exercise yields largely pat commentaries that reflect none of the energy we have seen in class.

Using purple ink, Alison writes in a painstakingly neat script that she interviewed "Emily, who practices the Jewish religion." She records Marysa's designated interview questions in aqua blue ("What is a basic belief of your religion?" "What is a major holiday?" "What is a special ceremony in your religion?" "What is a simple prayer?" and "What are the most important rules for good behavior?"), and transcribes Emily's answers in pink: "A basic belief is that there is one almighty God and someday he will come. He is the Messiah." And, "A special ceremony is a circumcision, when a baby boy's foreskin is removed from his penis. This is a sign of sanitation."

Chi-Ho's interview of Jim is similarly "neat," though less colorful. He writes in his journal: "Jim's religion is kind of similar to mine, because both believe in God and Jesus. . . . The basic belief of Catholics is that Jesus is the one who came to save us. We, the Protestants, usually have Bible Studies to learn about God and pray, but the Catholics have their ceremony without Bible Studies, but they pray and worship God. They have this every Sunday, like I do." Assiduously respectful, Chi-Ho's report on Jim reveals none of the negative value judgments warned against in the Facing History text. But another journal entry of Chi-Ho's implies that he may privately hold less tolerant attitudes. This other entry suggests that for some students at least, less socially acceptable feelings may indeed exist but be kept hidden from public expression—either in response to perceived social pressure or in deference to the class ground rules of respect. Commenting on the antisemitism expressed in *The Boy of Old Prague*, Chi-Ho writes: "If people hate the Jews, it should end up by hating them and boycotting their products or people, not killing and massacring them. Killing does not mean anything but losing, because it means you can not win over them by fair means. . . . Anti-semitism should not be violent but peaceful and unviolent. When you hate Jews you can discriminate, but not by physical way."

Though Chi-Ho raises an important point about degrees of discrimination, I have no doubt that Marysa and the Facing History program would take issue with his proposed "unviolent" alternative. Chi-Ho's decision to record these opinions in his journal may suggest his acquiescence to perceived classroom constraints (he chooses a private written dialogue with Marysa over a more public discussion with his peers), or, alternatively, his unwillingness to have his feelings silenced altogether (he chooses to share them with Marysa despite her potential censure). However, it is just as likely that Chi-Ho's entry simply reflects a lack of self-critical awareness: genuinely interested in finding "peaceful" and "fair means" for resolving differences, he seems unaware that hating Jews *simply because they are Jews* is itself problematic, whatever the means chosen to express it. By implicitly condoning discrimination, Chi-Ho may be living proof of Yoshi's earlier journal comment: "People tend not to see their own prejudices."

Facing History negotiates difficult terrain in attempting to reveal prejudice to students while encouraging their acceptance of multiple points of view. Students enter the classroom with different faiths and varying degrees of religious understanding. Marysa, Steve, and the Facing History *Resource Book* seek to provide answers to their religious questions without favoring a particular religious viewpoint. One could, I suppose, find fault with this position, for by assuming the relativity of faith, FHAO implicitly calls into question the absolute truth of any one religious doctrine. As we will see later, some critics of moral education have faulted Facing History and similar programs for precisely this reason.

As I see it, however, questioning absolute truth does not legitimate relativism as an alternative. Within the classroom community, a full range of students' religious beliefs are tolerated and brought into play; what is not tolerated are "putdowns of other people" and "not showing respect." Students are encouraged to condemn discriminatory attitudes, at the same time acknowledging difference. As Steve Cohen noted in class, in this chapter and others "[students] are going to look again and again at the things [they] believe in and ask [themselves], 'Why do I believe in that?'" The intent is neither to have students uncritically accept all beliefs nor to compel them to *change* their own; it is to help them *clarify* and stake a claim to their beliefs, cognizant of their impact on a diverse human community.

Not surprisingly, students respond differently to their encounter with differing truths. Those who enter the classroom clear in their beliefs seem untroubled by multiple points of view and others' religious questioning. Duane takes in the variety of opinions expressed in class but still concludes confidently, "I feel that [Jehovah's Witness] is the true religion and everybody should be following it. But, then again, there's other religions in the world and people feel like that's the right religion, so they may do so." And Melody responds matter-of-factly to Jess's query, "Why does everyone assume God is a man?" with "Because he got Mary pregnant! And since Jesus Christ is white, they also know God is white!" Melody listens closely to Jess's dissatisfaction with her answer but appears unfazed.

Students less certain of where they stand have a more difficult time tolerating multiple religious perspectives. Nata, Alan, and

Jamal transpose uncertainty onto an either-or framework: if multiple truths can be said to coexist, then any single claim must be invalid. Seeking to "complicate students' simple answers to complex problems,"[5] Steve counters Nata's charge that religion is "all lies" (or, at the very least, "exaggerated") by stressing the importance of understanding one's own beliefs and respecting those of others: "Well, some [religious] stories may be exaggerated, but the more important point is simply that people believe these things to be true. . . . Faith is going to be very important to think about in this course. We're not going to tell you this faith is right and this faith is wrong. Nobody can argue that your belief in God is any better or worse than anyone else's belief in God. That's something to think about." So if FHAO refuses to "answer" complex religious questions by championing any one religious doctrine, it does project a clear and consistent moral message: diversity exists and must be tolerated.

The clarity of this message must, in part, account for students' abilities to converse with each other despite significant differences across the religious spectrum, ranging from Duane's devout faith to Abby's bold atheism. In fact, these classroom sessions were remarkably uncontentious—no matter what their religious perspective, students remained more or less open to each other and themselves throughout class. By "open" I do not mean to suggest that students' willingly *ceded* their own individual beliefs, but rather that they willingly *tested* them through listening to each other and dialoguing together. This emotional and psychological process is not always easy, and the fact that this attempt produced neither hysterics nor polarization is itself an achievement. This outcome is by no means guaranteed, and it may be explained in light of curricular intention as well as conducive environmental factors.

In terms of the curriculum itself, it is important to recognize that this chapter of the FHAO text deals with a fictionalized historical account of religious prejudice (*The Boy of Old Prague*), and it is only through that highly distanced (and thus psychologically safe) account that students are asked to address their own assumptions, attitudes, and behaviors. Curriculum developers and Facing History teachers argue that this gap between present reality and historical events enables students to face issues of racism and prejudice in their own lives more openly than they would if the course was immediately focused on them. The text states: "After reading *The Boy of Old Prague*, students can relate the lessons on discrimination and prejudice to their own experiences in labeling and bias. And because the setting is another time and place in history it creates a distance that enables the student to speak more openly about the rumors, suspicions, and fears that they may have about Jewish people today. Often, though, class discussions are about other group hatreds. In many classes discussion about stereotyping of races different than their own begins here."[6]

My own classroom observations appear to bear this out: most students readily comprehend religious difference when it remains on a purely cognitive level. Admittedly, it is more difficult for students to apply historical lessons to their own lives than it is for them to understand a distanced historical subject. As Chi-Ho's journal entry suggests, gaps inevitably exist between certain cognitive understandings and personally held attitudes and beliefs. And, while none of Chi-Ho's classmates revealed such gaps in understanding, their journal reflections were often similarly lacking in critical self-reflection: most students had a far easier time identifying the prejudicial beliefs of their friends, family, and neighbors than their own. Students' responses to this chapter thus do and do not fulfill curricular expectations. Building on cognitive understanding, their comments and journal entries signify positive steps toward learning to listen to others and toward examining their own behavior in light of that listening. That these steps are small, at times uneven, and incremental is perhaps inevitable.

School Culture

Class discussion of this curricular topic was also aided by classroom and school culture. Marysa and Betty Lou's students knew (and by and large trusted) each other before being asked to speak publicly about sensitive issues related to their personal lives. Some students had been together at least seven months before the course broached the subject of respecting diverse religious perspectives and acknowledging the multicultural nature of truth; others had been together over a year and a half. The "ground rules" Marysa laid down at the start of the first day's discussion reflected not only the values of the Facing History course, but also the values of the Open Program and the Medgar Evers school itself. These values were present to students on a daily basis—from the civil rights legacy evoked by the school's name, engraved above the doors through which students entered the building each morning, to the colorful posters proclaiming "a world of difference" that papered school halls, to the explicit calls for respecting diversity voiced in school assemblies and classroom sessions. As Marysa herself noted, the multiculturally tolerant atmosphere I witnessed during this and other discussions of difference was something they had "been working very, very hard to develop."

As with the earlier class session described, students' ability to listen to each other and to reflect critically must be attributed not only to the Facing History curriculum, but also to the supportive groundwork laid by the classroom community and the school as a whole. The program would, no doubt, facilitate student's critical reflection in less sympathetic learning environments, but since students' classrooms are never sealed off from the rest of the school, and since schools are never sealed off from the rest of students' lives, the webs of support that exist between these environments may usefully further the distinct objectives of each.

Students struck me as being cognizant of how their school environment elicited and validated diverse points of view. In the course of our interviews, I asked students a number of questions explicitly linking Facing History course content with their school culture; in answer to these questions, students contrasted their own experience to that of the indoctrinated, obedient school children of Nazi Germany. A comment that Amiri made during an interview conveys a sentiment expressed by many students:

I guess [Hitler] was telling [German citizens] what they wanted to hear, and then once they heard that, they weren't really thinking for themselves anymore. They didn't really have their own mind of thinking, so they just believed everything that he said, and they never thought if it was right or not. . . . And [the Nazi children] were being taught not really to be an individual, and to give their life for their country and Hitler. They were taught that all Jewish people, and people other than themselves, were bad. And I guess they learned that Aryans were the best. . . . The [Medgar Evers school] has a different way of teaching people. They want you to be an individual, to think for yourself. . . . The Nazi teachers, they just gave the children lectures, and they told them what to do, and they weren't allowed to ask any questions at all! Whatever they said was just true! And that's not true at this school 'cause a lot of times here, there are disagreements with what other people are saying, and I mean, you can ask questions. . . . That happens about every day! People are always arguing with the teacher, not only about things that she's teaching, but other things, you know. They don't just get everything just from the books. They don't believe, we don't believe, everything we hear.

The kind of education that Amiri describes—education that encourages students to think for themselves, test their hypotheses, question each other, and remain in dialogue—is arguably the kind of education needed to create individuals capable of autonomous and critical moral reasoning. The Medgar Evers school and the Facing History and Ourselves program clearly convey certain values to students and set clear moral parameters for what constitutes socially acceptable behavior; students in these classrooms have been encouraged to refrain from discrimination and to treat each other with respect, for example. But the specific values conveyed through this program are no more important than the mental process students are engaged in, a process whereby students learn how to think through conflicting moral claims and viewpoints on their own. Facing History does not so much provide students with a particular set of beliefs (it does not, for example, tell them which religious beliefs to uphold) as it trains them how to think through complex issues, like religious doctrine, for themselves. This type of education is of course concerned that students grasp the lessons of history, literature, and other fundamental subject matter, but it is at least equally concerned that they develop mental habits that will help them sustain autonomous moral reasoning when teachers, parents, or other moral mentors are not around. The type of education that Amiri describes is, arguably, *civic* education. Teachers of the Facing History program hope it will help students reason their way through conflicts arising from differing beliefs (religious or otherwise) that they encounter daily in their classroom, and that they will eventually encounter in the world at large.

Chapter Four

"Confronting What Is Hard to Think About"

It is an unseasonably hot day in May. Students sit fanning themselves with their spiral notebooks as late-morning sun pours into the classroom through a large, partially closed window on the far side of the room. Nursing her latest sports injury, Jess limps to her seat clad in navy blue shorts and an oversized University of Michigan T-shirt. Abby sports a summer-bright turquoise shirt, matching socks, and white stretch pants. The top piece of her shoulder-length, sandy-blond hair is pulled back in a clip, and her bangs remain loose and hanging. Sandra's clothing and hairstyle are almost identical. Marlene looks smart in her denim miniskirt and matching pink cotton sweater, pink hair elastic, pink socks, and fingernails whose pinkish-red polish is beginning to chip. Most other students are in shorts and tennis shoes.

It is the eleventh and second-to-last week of the Facing History and Ourselves course. The few classes left are intended to help students transition from World War II to the present. Using students' understanding of the Holocaust as a lens through which to approach more immediate concerns, Marysa focuses the remaining class discussions around contemporary political problems in order to highlight students' own social and political responsibilities. This way of bringing closure to the course is in keeping with the final chapter of the Facing History *Resource Book*:

> This curriculum must provide opportunities for students to explore the practical applications of freedom, which they have learned demand a constant struggle with difficult, controversial, and com-

plex issues. The responsibility that citizens have for one another as neighbors and as nations cannot be left to others. This history has taught that there is no one else to confront terrorism, ease the yoke and pain of racism, attack apathy, create and enforce just laws, and wage peace but *us*. . . . We need practice in confronting what is hard to think about. We believe that participating in decision-making about difficult and controversial issues gives practice in listening to different opinions, deciphering fact from opinion, confronting emotion and reason, negotiating, and problem-solving. In the political arena, where ideas compete with each other for support, choosing a side ensures against apathy and encourages political participation.[1]

Marysa circulates around the uncomfortably hot classroom handing out the syllabus for the week. Listing all reading and homework assignments for the next five days, the syllabus begins with a quote from radical community organizer Saul Alinsky that is directly relevant to this week's discussion. Laid out across the top of the page are his words: "Change means movement, movement means friction, friction means heat, and heat means controversy. The only place where there is no friction is in outer space or a seminar on political action."

Intended as a comment on political conflicts in the world at large, Alinsky's remark proves equally telling about classroom dynamics. Over the next several days, students will view provocative documentary films about individuals and/or organizations holding controversial and differing political beliefs. These films (and related readings) are intended to impress on students the importance of clarifying one's own political beliefs and raise complex questions about how a democratic and pluralistic society should best handle the conflicts generated by political diversity. As students discuss these films, political differences within the classroom itself will be illuminated and debated, and dilemmas raised by the course's intellectual content will be mirrored in the lived curriculum of classroom dynamics.

From my perspective, these classroom dynamics reveal tensions about conflicting values and ideologies among teachers, students, and the Facing History curriculum itself, demonstrating the enormous complexity of the endeavor to catalyze critical, moral thinking among adolescent students. On the one hand, the FHAO program advocates bringing forth multiple points of view, developing students' understanding of multiple perspectives, and promoting tolerance among diverse peoples of often differing backgrounds. In the classes I have observed, teacher practice is to a considerable extent in keeping with these curricular values; teachers often actively engage with students of diverse political perspectives and encourage them to remain fair-minded and open to at least hearing alternative points of view. On the other hand, program teachers unequivocally reject moral relativism, condemning social attitudes and beliefs that in any way repress or discriminate against social groups.

Tensions inevitably arise when teachers and students differ in their feelings about which beliefs actually further or hinder these stated curricular objectives. Whose standards should determine what is morally "right" or "wrong"? Do these determinations align with an individual's own political beliefs? How should beliefs that some regard as "wrong" be handled in the classroom? What are the repercussions of silencing these viewpoints, or, alternatively, allowing them to be voiced freely? These questions are increasingly the subject of national educational debate.

Marysa and her students clearly struggle with questions such as these. A close look at how they are dealt with here—within the safety of a trusted school community—may help to illuminate how they are negotiated within a broader social context. It may also shed light on the controversies that have raged around moral education curricula historically, and around the Facing History and Ourselves curriculum in particular.

Movement Means Friction

"Remember yesterday? What did we see?" Marysa asks about a film in which the subject of political difference is raised. Sandra answers,

"A story about a man who taught his students that the Holocaust never happened, and that Jews wanted to rule the world." Abby adds, "He also said that all the banks and the finances were controlled by Jewish people." "Yeah," agrees Alan, "he thought there was an international Jewish conspiracy."

Students take turns passionately describing *Lessons in Hate*, an early-1980s documentary about Jim Keegstra, a popular and charismatic mayor and teacher in a small town in Alberta, Canada, who taught antisemitic beliefs to his all-white students for more than a decade. The film extensively documents Keegstra arguing that the Holocaust was a "hoax" that in no way singled out Jewish people. He also argues that the French Revolution was a product of the "international Jewish conspiracy"; that John Wilkes Booth, the man who shot Abraham Lincoln, was a Jew; and that Jews caused the American Civil War. Young, vulnerable, and with little access to alternative beliefs or perspectives, Keegstra's students uncritically absorbed his teachings, or, in a few cases, adopted them ambivalently in order to receive a passing grade. More problematic still, Keegstra's statements were tacitly accepted by the school's principal and faculty, and by most of the town council and citizens. When the mother of one student finally challenged Keegstra's teachings, she was vehemently opposed by members of her community. The school board eventually fired Keegstra, but not until after a long and difficult battle had been waged that painfully divided members of the small town.[2] True to Alinsky's comment, the battle caused fury, confusion, and "friction."

The Keegstra film raises questions about how a community can tolerate conflictual beliefs among its members while still maintaining cohesion. Showcasing the struggles experienced by both Keegstra and those who oppose him, it demonstrates how difficult it can be to stand up for one's beliefs, regardless of their content. After what they have read, seen, and been taught throughout the semester, Marysa's students are outraged that anyone could minimize the horror of the Holocaust, much less deny its very existence. Distancing themselves from their Canadian peers, some make disparaging remarks about Keegstra's seemingly docile and gullible students. Marysa reminds the class: "It's like that quote by Hitler that we talked about earlier in the course—'If you tell a lie big enough and long enough, people will believe you.' Well, for fourteen years, Mr. Keegstra told his students what to him was an absolute truth, and people believed it!"

> *Abby:* It seems like these people just feed on people who are torn apart. They just suck them up by providing them with an excuse to hate! They probably want to find a way to place the blame on someone else just to explain their own situation.
>
> *Marysa:* Exactly! What's the vocabulary word which describes that? (Several students shout out, *scapegoating.*) Well, what can you do to help people when they're in this condition? What can you do to turn their beliefs around?
>
> *Josh:* Kill them!
>
> *Marysa:* What?! Kill them?!
>
> *Josh:* Yes. If they say those things, and if they start a war or something, you have to fight back.
>
> *Alan:* But if you go out and fight these people, and you kill 600 or 700 of them, it won't stop anything! More will just come and fight back!

Encouraging her students to remain cognizant of their own values and beliefs in light of pressure to do otherwise, Marysa responds: "What I'm really trying to push is that this is not just a problem that happened in history, a long time ago—the Dark Ages, when I was born. These issues are here, in the present. And you're a part of it. You have to be aware of it so you are not brainwashed or indoctrinated in the future. . . . We have what we perceive as an excellent system of education in this country, universally open to everybody. But in some places, even in our own country, that's not what people want."

For the next several minutes, students discuss the apparent differences between their own multicultural community and Keegstra's ethnically homogeneous school and town. Marysa asks students to identify similarities between Nazi doctrine and what Keegstra taught, and Abby brings up the international Jewish conspiracy theme. Drawing this argument closer to home, Marysa suggests parallels between the historical claim that Jews have controlled the financial industry and the present-day fear that Japanese increasingly dominate the U.S. economy. Chi-Ho raises his hand and quietly drops a bombshell: "I think that a Jewish international conspiracy does exist, but not quite as much they say. So many people are talking about it, it must be some way true." "What?!" several students exclaim at once. Josh stares in disbelief at the boy who sits next to him, suddenly a stranger. Susie and Jess, incredulous at Chi-Ho's statement, yell out simultaneously. Marysa responds in a strained but consciously even-tempered voice, "Chi-Ho, why do you think this?" Chi-Ho answers in a somewhat muffled voice, "I don't know, but I do." Marysa continues, "Don't you think that if there was a conspiracy it could have stopped the Holocaust?" "No, I don't," Chi-Ho replies, "because it's more recent. It's developed since the 1950s only, I think." Marysa responds emphatically, "Chi-Ho, we need to talk!"

Animated one-on-one conversations spring up between students who sit next to each other in all corners of the room; the whole class seems to be buzzing. Abby raises her hand and (deliberately or not) turns up the heat several notches. She says, "I'm against what some people are doing with Israel, with the way it was established and with killing the Palestinians and everything. But that's different from an international Jewish conspiracy." "What are you talking about?" Josh exclaims furiously. "We weren't even talking about that!" Sandra adds critically, "What are you against now, Abby?" Abby answers, "I'm against the way the country was set up." Marysa asks incredulously and slightly sarcastically, "The UN vote?" Abby replies, "Not that, but what happened to the Palestinian people through that. Elie Wiesel and people like that were involved, and millions of Palestinian people were massacred and forced to leave their homes, just like in the Holocaust."

All hell breaks loose. It seems like everyone begins yelling at Abby, and Chi-Ho's earlier remark is left by the wayside. Abby steadfastly holds her ground. Though her words remain strong and her claims unqualified, she slumps further and further into her seat with each new attack of her classmates. She strikes me as being both scared and defiant. Confused about historical facts, Josh defends the state of Israel:

Josh: They were attacked in an eight-day war!
Abby: Well, it's still not right to be killing people to set up a country!
Josh: That's exactly what we did to set up our country!
Abby: So? I'm against that, too! I don't believe in that either!
Sandra: (Becoming increasingly exasperated) Well, what are you for? What do you believe in? (Alison and Susie nod emphatically in agreement.)
Abby: (Matter-of-factly) I believe in control by the people.
Marysa: But how do you determine which people should have control, Abby? In the film we saw, the Canadian teacher thinks he should have control, because he thinks he's right. How are you going to decide who gets to speak and who doesn't?

Students debate the conundrum of free speech for the remaining few minutes of class. Though Marysa has (perhaps self-consciously) shifted discussion away from a contentious and personalized debate, the classroom atmosphere remains charged.

I am scheduled to interview Abby later on this same day. As students get ready for lunch, I watch Abby self-consciously gather her books, seeming proud yet uncomfortable about being isolated. Calling out to her, I suggest that during our interview, we can discuss the points she has raised in class, if she is interested; she smiles appreciatively. Sandra, Alison, and Angela note my overture and come up to speak with me on their way out of the room.

"Look, I don't know much about the Jewish religion, or any religion, really," Sandra says, "but isn't it true that in the Bible it says that the land was originally Jewish land, and that's why they wanted it? Or, why didn't the Jewish people just go to a different country?" I try to answer as best as I can, explaining that Jews, Christians, and Moslems have all lived on this land, and that all have laid claim to it in different periods of history. "But doesn't the Bible say that the Jews were there first?" Angela retorts, "And then the Moslems came when the Jews went to Egypt?" Trying to grant each group its legitimacy, I speak to the importance of finding contemporary political solutions to the problem. Seeing myself more as a participant/observer than an arbiter of diverging viewpoints, I refuse to choose sides despite the girls' best efforts to make me do so. The three girls head off for lunch less angry, but still visibly confused.

Josh leaves class upset by the comments made by both Abby and Chi-Ho. He speaks to Marysa for almost an hour after class, refusing to sit next to Chi-Ho and demanding that his seat be changed. In keeping with the curriculum's intent to foster students' ability to listen to alternative perspectives, Marysa tells me later, "I tried to explain to Josh that Chi-Ho was the same person Josh thought he was before he made that statement. I told him that the way to respond to problems is not to refuse to speak to someone, but to talk together to try to figure it out and to help people to change their beliefs."

But "talking together" is not always easy. True to Alinsky's comment, "frictions" caused by Abby and Chi-Ho seem to circulate around the class as a whole (several students shout at Abby and Chi-Ho), between students and their teacher (Marysa expresses unequivocal disapproval of both students' comments), and, perhaps most poignantly, within students' individual relationships. Josh says of Chi-Ho after class:

> He's been my friend all year and he stands up and says, "I believe in the Jewish international conspiracy, I don't think they do everything that they say they do, but I think there is one." And you know [Josh makes an exasperated sound], he's sitting right next to me! . . . You

know, I looked at him, and he wouldn't look at me. I could tell he was so embarrassed . . . I said, "Look at me! Do you really believe that?" He kind of looked down and nodded. And he pulled out this dollar bill and said, "See, look at the eye . . . that represents Jews looking over the world."

Chi-Ho says of Josh, "I think he totally misunderstood! He thought I am against him! And I didn't mean to say that! All I meant is that there is something like an economical conspiracy, and it may have some control, some banks, and would try to compete against Japan, but it's not totally by Jews, and I didn't say that it was authorized by Jews, but I think, I think Josh thought that I said so."

Sandra also expresses frustration with Abby. Angered by what she perceives as Abby's self-righteous air and resentful of feeling pressured by her, Sandra says somewhat vengefully, "[Abby] was trying to get me to believe what she was thinking, so I could back her up! And I wasn't sure, and I said, 'Well, I'm not sure!' And she goes, 'But it was like this!' And I was like, 'Don't say it to me, you know, say it to [the teacher!].' . . . I'd kind of got sick of hearing what she was always like, 'this is what I read in the book,' and everything."

Marysa leaves class as upset as many of her students and uncertain about how to proceed. In fact, her confusion seems to have been manifest in her classroom dealings. Confronted with views she finds repugnant and even dangerous, she does, nevertheless, encourage students to remain open-minded, independent in their thinking, and respectful of difference. "These issues are here, in the present. And you're a part of it," she reminds her class. "You have to be aware of it so you are not brainwashed or indoctrinated in the future." At the same time, however, Marysa implicitly undermines those views with which she disagrees. Though this is rather subtly accomplished, I find it problematic, nonetheless.

While perhaps not done consciously, Marysa utilizes the power implicit in her authority as classroom teacher to delegitimize Chi-Ho's and Abby's perspectives. In keeping with curricular principles, Marysa in no way *openly* silences the students in her class. On the contrary, she engages Abby and Chi-Ho in a critical debate, urging them to clarify their thinking and to defend their controversial points of view. But given the power differential between teacher and student, this debate is unevenly weighted. Though Marysa teaches in the Open Program and is called by her first name, she remains "the teacher," empowered to design seating plans, assign homework, give grades, and arbitrate conflicts. Publicly acknowledging her disagreement with both students, Marysa uses her implicit authority to undermine, rather than muzzle, their perspectives.

For example, Marysa challenges Chi-Ho's remarks before the full classroom community, but then seeks to remove them from the public arena. "Chi-Ho, we need to talk," she says after only a brief exchange, simultaneously displacing disagreement to the private realm and suggesting that, once there, she will set the record straight. Moments later, Marysa chooses not to intervene when several students jump on Abby, and her own questions of Abby sound slightly facetious. When Abby notes she is "against the way [Israel] was set up," Marysa asks incredulously "The UN vote?," suggesting by her tone that this is a nonpolitical body and beyond reproof. Finally, Marysa eventually steers discussion away from the Middle East and toward freedom of speech in the midst of an unresolved debate.

Admittedly uncomfortable with the arguments raised and feeling unequipped to handle them, Marysa avails herself of her proximity to the Facing History and Ourselves national office and calls in staff member Steve Cohen to address the controversial issues raised by Abby and Chi-Ho. By now well known and well liked by most of the class, Steve comes in a few days later for "damage control." It is a slightly cooler day.

Friction Means Heat

"Why did Hitler choose to focus on the Jews?" Steve asks to open this morning's complex agenda. Alan replies, "He said that they were in charge of the money." Jess adds, "He said they were the people who put Germany in the economic state they were in." "Well, why did people believe it?" Steve continues. Abby: "It's like that quote. If you tell a lie big enough and long enough, people will start to believe it." Steve: "Do you think that's true, from your own experience?" "Well, I've always been someone who doesn't like to just go along with what other people are saying," Abby replies, "but yeah, if you hear something long enough, it affects you . . . you kind of forget what your own principles are."

Steve bounces around the room, weaving around students' desks and speaking quickly in an animated voice often squeaky with excitement. Focusing directly on each student with whom he speaks and referring to each by name, he engages the class in a discussion about how basic emotions and stereotypes take over when you "forget your own principles" and are "no longer able to think." "I want you to think about how stereotypes and propaganda work," Steve explains, "because, as you know, Hitler doesn't invent anything new. Before Hitler, there was plenty of hatred of Jews." He continues with the following example:

In the 1890s, a book appeared, and it was called . . . *Protocols of the Elders of Zion*. [Steve writes the title of the book on the board, and students copy it into their journals.] It appeared in Russian in 1890. And it explained that there was an international group of Jews who used to get together and meet in a Jewish cemetery in Prague, at night, and they would plan everything that was going to happen in the world. [Josh taps Chi-Ho on the shoulder, as if to suggest that he should listen closely.] This book was republished in England in 1919. It was republished in the U.S. in the 1920s—in a newspaper owned by Henry Ford, one of the two or three most important men in the country! In England it was published in *the* most important newspaper—the *Times* of London. And the most interesting thing about this book is—it's a fraud! It's complete nonsense! It's made up! [Josh again prods Chi-Ho and whispers something to him; Chi-Ho smiles awkwardly.] How do you know it's a fraud? Well, in the 1890s, this book was written by members of the Russian police force. [Steve writes "1890—Russian police force" hurriedly on the board.] And how do you know that? Well, because this book was actually copied [Steve's voice cracks in excitement] from a book that was written in 1864 in France that didn't blame Jews, but that said the ruler of France, Napoleon the Third, was trying to take over the world [he writes "Napoleon, 1864" on the board]. And everywhere where Napoleon appears in this book [Steve points to the original text], the word *Jews* appears in this one [he points to the words "Elders of Zion"]. Think about this for a second! A French book in 1864 was copied by the Russians in 1890. The British copied the Russians. And the Americans copied the British. And it's a complete fraud! It's hocus pocus! It's untrue! It's a *lie*. And millions and millions of people believed it. [Pause.] How come?

Susie: Because nobody told them any differently.
Alan: Because they believed it was written by someone who knew!
Josh: A lot of people want to blame somebody else for all of their problems.
Chi-Ho: Because then you're not responsible for what happens to people.

"Exactly!" Steve exclaims. "There are a lot of things that happen that are really beyond our control. An idea like this says—even if it's someone you hate, somebody is in control. Somebody is in charge of what's going on. And even if things are lousy, it's nice to be able to say, it wouldn't be lousy if it weren't for these bums. Let me show you how this happened in real life! This should take about five hours, but I'll do it in three minutes. You ready?" Students nod that they are.

For the next several minutes, Steve gives a remarkably clear and concise account of the infamous turn-of-the-century case in which Alfred Dreyfus, one of the few Jewish officers in the French Army, was falsely accused of giving military secrets to the Germans, convicted in two trials, and sentenced to prison on Devil's Island. "Many people said, 'How could Dreyfus have done it alone?' And others said, 'Aha, he didn't! He was part of this!' " [Steve points again to "Elders of Zion" on the board].

>*Abby:* Is that thing called the international Jewish conspiracy?
>*Steve:* In France, they called it the "Syndicat." And they referred
>   to it as the "international Jewish conspiracy." There's a
>   tremendous power in this kind of idea. Why were people so
>   willing to believe it of Jews? Would they have believed it if
>   this was . . . about Catholics? Would that have been popular
>   in Europe?

"No," answers Sandra, "there are a lot of Catholics, so it wouldn't be as easy as singling out one Jew." Nodding his head in agreement, Steve adds: "This notion of the majority and the minority is really powerful. If you are in the majority in a society, then you pretty much set the rules. The power of rulers is really something. Have any of you ever believed a ruler that you later found out was untrue? Or believed something you found out later wasn't true? What I'm about to tell you is probably the truest thing I ever learned: write it down! It's not the things you don't know that hurt you. It's the things you do know that aren't so."

Students corroborate Steve's point by providing different examples of things people have thought they knew that later turned out to be false. Alan brings up the Iran-Contra affair. Amiri and Marlene bring up the Charles Stuart murder case.[3] Abby interjects, "What things you believe in will also depend on the family you grow up in." Steve agrees, and draws today's first thorny agenda item to a close by reinforcing the curriculum's valuation of critical thinking. He says: "One of the things you're going to have to decide is whether you're going to believe what people say, or whether you're going to try to figure it out on your own."

Chi-Ho has remained almost completely silent throughout this discussion. Often quiet in class, his behavior today is not unusual.

Today's lecture, however, is given in response to his earlier remark, and it would seem to call for his participation. While only Josh makes a point of publicly acknowledging the connection between the previous class and today's (by tugging at Chi-Ho's shirtsleeve and whispering to him repeatedly), other students shoot furtive glances in Chi-Ho's direction. Chi-Ho seems to studiously ignore all meaningful looks. Though he appears to be listening throughout class and assiduously copies Steve's chalkboard notes into his journal, he does not acknowledge that today's lecture was, however subtly, directed at him.

This is by no means the case with Abby when the second item on today's agenda is discussed. Referring to a set of maps of the pre– and post–World War I period, Steve shows how the world has changed since the fall of the Ottoman Empire. He points to the Middle East region and says: "There are white people, black people, and brown people living here. It's a whole Rainbow Coalition! After World War I, one of the major questions was—should people like this be able to rule themselves? And the winners of the war—France, Britain, and the U.S.—say 'No!' They give them independence with training wheels, and the winners of the war are gonna be the training wheels! These people end up living in countries that are *invented* after World War I. It's all a product of politics! Well, what kinds of problems might the 'training wheels' encounter?"

"They had to make sure the new boundaries wouldn't get people mad because they don't want to start another war," Alan answers thoughtfully. Nora adds, "They needed to keep people together with their own people so they'll be content." Drawing his finger across a large section of the map, Steve describes how Transjordan was ruled by the victorious British until 1948. "And who lived here?" he asks simply, pointing to Palestine.

Abby: Palestinians.
Steve: Who were they, and what was their religion?
Abby: They were Arabs.

Steve: They were Moslems, Jews, and Christians. To be a
"Palestinian" meant literally to live in Palestine. And they
all lived under British rule.

For the next several minutes, Steve helps the class review what
happened to Jews in the years leading up to and immediately following World War II. Josh remembers that Jews tried to get out of
Europe but often had no place to go. Angela believes many headed
for Palestine because they had "religious ties there." Nora comments
that it was often impossible to return to their homes because "they
were taken by people like their neighbors." Zeke adds that their pos-
sessions were taken, too.

"Lots of Jews live in detention camps for two or three years after
the war," Steve explains. "The Jews in Palestine want the European
Jews to come there, but the Arabs and Christians don't want them
to. The British have control of Palestine and they don't know what
to do with it. Since the British can't figure it out, they give the
problem to the UN, which functions as an international government with representatives from different countries. This is the UN's
big moment! Well, in 1947 the UN votes to divide Palestine again,
into a state for Jews and a state for non-Jews."

"Is this when the eight-day war took place?" Josh interjects,
reviving his previous comment. "No," Steve answers, "that took
place later." Nora comments, "The UN is made up of representatives from all different countries, right? So, what did the Palestinian
representative do?" Supportive and genuinely impressed, Steve
exclaims, "That's a great question! There wasn't one since Palestine
was under British rule." "Well," Nora continues, "did the majority of
the non-Jews in Palestine agree with the decision?" Steve responds,
"Absolutely not! The majority of people were not happy. So in 1948
a war occurs—it's a small war compared to World War I and World
War II—and in that war, the *Jewish* side of Palestine manages to survive, but the *non-Jewish* portion gets taken—not by Israel, but by
'Transjordan' . . . the Jewish part becomes Israel, but the non-Jewish
part becomes Jordan and Egypt."

Abby is getting frustrated with Steve's version of history. She breaks in in a loud and exasperated voice, "But there was lots of violence between the Jews and non-Jews! A lot of people were killed! People were kicked off their homes. It was just like in the Holocaust!" Steve acknowledges the complexity of the situation but is direct in his rebuttal. Calmly and with authority, he asserts, "That's not quite true; part of it's true, but it's very complex. There were broadcasts telling people to leave their land, and many people wanted to leave because they wanted to get away from the war. When the Israeli government came in, they didn't know what to do with the Arab land. The people that fled their homes do end up living in camps, but that's the choice of the Jordanians, not the Israelis." Abby objects, saying, "But they shouldn't have had to leave in the first place!" "They chose to leave," Steve responds.

> There's no question that this displaced people and that people lost their homes who didn't want to. But there's also no question that extermination was not the policy. . . . The other thing is that many Jews in these Arab countries also lost their homes. One of the things that happens in times of war is that international human rights are completely neglected. This should make us think very closely about the policies of international government—they're not extermination policies, but they're also not policies that make it very easy for people to live their lives in the way they would like to.

Abby isn't satisfied. "But if the Palestinians hadn't been kicked off . . ." she begins. Steve breaks in, "Do you mean the Palestinian non-Jews?" Accommodating Steve's language, Abby continues, "OK, if the Palestinian non-Jews hadn't been kicked off, why should they be so angry about not having their land?" "Oh, well! They've spent the past forty years living in camps and wanting to be on their parents' land!" Steve responds.

Most students have remained silent yet attentive during this exchange. Sandra sits close to Abby and does not come to her aid despite Abby's frequent, beseeching looks in her direction. Josh only half hides a smirk, seemingly pleased that Steve is taking Abby on. He now contributes to the discussion: "But there was another war!" Steve replies, "There have been lots of wars. The tension Abby speaks to developed more after the land was taken in 1967. Many people believe that land should be exchanged for peace. There's a large Peace Now movement in Israel today saying that those territories should be given back to the Palestinian Arabs."

"But they won the war!" Josh repeats emphatically. "I learned that in Temple!" Steve responds by briefly highlighting different points of view within contemporary Israeli (Jewish) society. He is careful to distinguish between current policies and those on which the state was founded. Though he admits the existence of conflicting perspectives within contemporary Israeli society ("Many people believe that land should be exchanged for peace"), he leaves less room for alternative interpretation when it comes to the founding of the state ("The tension Abby speaks to developed more after the land was taken in 1967," he says, and he suggests that Palestinians were not "kicked off" their land, but "chose" to leave it). Though Steve is by no means alone in articulating this perspective (and in distinguishing it from current Israeli policies), it nonetheless reflects only one particular viewpoint in a complex and contentious historical debate.[4]

Some of Steve's other interventions are also grounded in a particular political stance. While acknowledging that the founding of the State of Israel was accompanied by some human rights violations, he denies that those violations were systematic or a matter of official policy. Moments later, he "corrects" Abby's language by recommending that she refer to Arabs as "Palestinian non-Jews"—a categorization that is itself not politically neutral, and arguably comparable to referring to blacks as nonwhites or women as nonmen. Like Marysa in the earlier classroom incident, Steve acts in somewhat contradictory ways, eliciting students' diverse viewpoints on the one hand while undermining the legitimacy of those with which he disagrees on the other.

Class nearly over, students begin to close their notebooks and put them inside their desks. Marysa and Steve turn to each other and begin speaking privately in the front of the room; they express pleasure and relief at having gotten through a potentially difficult session without drawing too much fire.

That neither Steve nor Marysa entirely transcended their own political beliefs in interpreting and responding to political differences within the classroom is not surprising; I would argue that no one can do so. These beliefs are a part of our internal makeup, as operative within these teachers as they are within my own interpretations of their practice. I did not leave my own political beliefs at the door when I entered the classroom; they were within me as I observed each class. These perspectives no doubt influenced how I interpreted classroom tensions between eliciting and muting student voices: I felt strongly opposed to Chi-Ho's remarks even as I disagreed with how they were handled, and I was partially supportive of some of Abby's comments, even as I objected to her more extreme claims as well as to how they were invalidated. The interpretations of students themselves might be an important corrective in this regard.

In fact, interviews conducted individually with Chi-Ho, Abby, Josh, and Sandra shortly after these classes took place support my interpretation of these classroom events as political in nature. By "political" I mean to suggest not only the content of the classroom debate (in which a diversity of political views were expressed) but also the process by which it was negotiated (whereby controversial voices were silenced by those with greater authority and power). In these instances, power was exercised between students and their teachers, between Marysa and Steve, and among the students themselves. So too, were the relations among these players hierarchical: some were given (or assumed) more authority to speak than others. And, depending on one's point of view, opposing positions were granted legitimacy or invalidated. In the process, some students felt silenced and subordinated, while others felt empowered and privileged.

In our interviews, Chi-Ho and Abby expressed discomfort at

feeling "unheard" and "misunderstood" in class, while Sandra and Josh enjoyed the fact that these students were silenced. Expressing frustration with being "misunderstood," Chi-Ho remarks: "[Josh] wouldn't listen! . . . [It felt] terrible . . . I was disappointed. I really think that Marysa didn't really listen to me very carefully, and, if she did, she would understand what I meant." Attempting to clarify his opinions to me because he felt precluded from doing so in class, Chi-Ho continues: "I'm not antisemitic. I can't be! I don't want to be. I can't just say that Jews are the bankers and they are responsible for the economy. I don't want to be like that! All I am saying is that there must be an economic conspiracy which will help loan money to the countries, European and America, to prevent Japan from growing too much farther."

Abby's response to the classes under study is multifaceted. She initially admits to being confused by Steve's alternative reading of historical events and expresses concern for (what she imagines to be) *his* discomfort. Portraying *herself* as the agent of her silencing (rather than Steve), Abby notes: "I really was confused by what he said, because, from what I had read (because my parents have a lot of books about that), it really was the total opposite of what he was saying. And, I mean, I didn't want to make a scene, so I didn't really, you know, say as much as I could have? I didn't want to totally contradict him, 'cause it would have made him feel uncomfortable. So I just kind of left it."

Moments later, however, Abby suggests that this self-censorship was not entirely voluntarily. Though she hesitantly adopts Steve's terminology, she nevertheless defends her own perspective and argues that he was unable to hear it:

> I thought about it a lot during and afterwards, and I really think that his point of view was really, really closed-minded! You know, he wouldn't think about, I mean, he thought about what I had to say, but he basically said it was totally wrong! . . . I was trying to tell him that from what I've learned, the situation between, um, Palestinian non-Jews, and the Jews was very oppressive, and one-sided, and, it

was really an awful situation! And he kind of glorified it in a way, and made it sound like it wasn't as violent as it really was!

While Abby eventually admits to having modified some of her own thinking in response to Steve, she seems frustrated that he has not done the same:

> I didn't really mean millions because there weren't that many Palestinian non-Jews in the country. But I mean, he was right, because I thought about it and it wasn't really extermination. But they really wanted them to move off that land! And it was their homeland in the first place! And I *meant* that by taking them out of their home, as the Nazis did with the Jews, they put them in something that was like a camp where they weren't allowed to have any human rights that most people take for granted. I agree with him that the methods weren't exactly extermination but I don't agree with him when he says it wasn't as bad as in the first steps [of the Holocaust].

By contrast, neither Josh nor Sandra express discomfort with classroom dynamics, but they express pleasure in Steve's having silenced those with whom they disagree. Sandra notes with satisfaction, "When Steve came in and told Abby 'You're wrong!' well, it was kind of funny, because she got like, really mad." Josh similarly notes, "Steve, he's great! He came in and he said this is total nonsense." Whispering "Don't tell her, but Abby talks a lot!" Josh takes pleasure in describing a contentious class in which his own beliefs reflect majority opinion while Abby's are seen as marginal: "She was talking, and she said that she didn't like Israel because of the way that they were founded, and that she'd throw the Jews out. And then everyone started yelling, 'Well how was this country founded?' And she said, 'Well, I don't like this country either!' And then everyone started yelling, 'Well, who are, what do you like!' I disagree with Abby a lot!" He says later of Steve's having put Chi-Ho in his place, "I like when people make sure people know what's going on."

These excerpts suggest a confluence between my interpretation of classroom dynamics and students' experience of the course. Though students differed among themselves in their feelings about classroom dynamics, they shared my belief that both Marysa and Steve conveyed their own sense of "right" and "wrong" to the class and made sure, as Josh says, that "people know what's going on."

Heat Means Controversy

The day after Steve Cohen's visit, students return to the issue of contemporary political conflicts as originally intended by the curricular text. Walking toward the back of the class with a videotape in hand, Marysa begins: "We've talked about the thirties and the forties, and we've seen a movie about something happening in Canada in the eighties. Now we're going to look at our own home, the U.S. This documentary film is about the Ku Klux Klan teaching kids your age.[5] Imagine if you grew up in a town, an all-black town, say, and you adored your teacher, and he told you all about all the horrible things whites did—many of which I think are true. Would it be easy to believe it?"

"It would be real easy," Jamal answers without hesitation, "'cause he'd be my role model."

"That's why indoctrination is so scary, and so important to understand," Marysa continues. "If you hear something again and again from someone you believe in, and you don't hear anything else, even though it may be one person's perspective, you'll probably believe it. . . . So in a way the diversity around you here, and the strengths from the differences of opinion you hear, and the strengths of the educational system you're in, encourage you to question and to learn different points of view. Try to think about that while you're watching this." Marysa pops the videocassette into the VCR, Angela hits the lights, and students settle down to watch TV. The film begins:

Hundreds of men wearing long white robes and pointed hats stand expectantly in a large, outdoor open area. It is nighttime, and a cross-lighting ceremony is about to begin. We watch as men set fire to a giant cross and cheer as it burns while a voice-over tells us this is Alabama, 1980, where Klan membership has doubled in the past five years. Now 10,000 people strong in twenty-two states, the Klan builds membership by actively recruiting and training a special youth division for ten- to seventeen-year-olds.

Scene two: row upon row of cleanly scruffed white boys and girls stand at attention and recite the Klan Youth Corps pledge. They chant in unison: "I pledge to practice racial separation in all my social contacts and to keep my forced contacts with other races on a strictly business basis. I pledge to oppose the false teaching that all races are equal or the same. I pledge that I will immediately go to the aid of any white person being attacked physically or verbally by a person of another race. I pledge that I will fight for the complete separation of all races in America and I will recruit others to do the same."

Randy, a pudgy white boy who looks to be about eleven or twelve, is interviewed by CBS-TV news correspondent Christopher Glenn. "Blacks aren't as intelligent as whites," Randy asserts with total conviction. "In school, walking down halls, they're going up and putting their arms around white girls. That's a mixture of the races, and that's not intelligent. . . . Black niggers, communists, the Jews, the Vietnamese and everybody is coming to America. The Klan means white supremacy."

For the next several minutes, we watch Randy and others like him in a Klan Youth summer camp. Here Youth Corps members swim, play ball, and, in between these harmless activities, receive structured lessons in Klan philosophy. "Many of the things you read in school are not the truth—they're just lies," a Klan counselor instructs a group of campers. The voice-over tells us that the Youth Corps has branches in six states; once trained and eighteen years of age, these youths become official members of the Ku Klux Klan.

The documentary crew next follows a Youth Corps group to a shopping mall near Birmingham, Alabama, where they hope to recruit new members. Klan youth hand out resource literature and speak with white passersby. While most white young people rebuff the Corps' initiatives, and a black teenage girl expresses pain and fury, a mother of two enthusiastically signs up her sons.

The camera pans back to another nighttime rally scene where the Klan's Imperial Wizard makes a stirring appeal: "We will kill. We will stand in the streets. We will do what we have to to stop the niggers and the communists, won't we? It's good to see people out there holding guns. America was built on the gun. The Bible and the gun carved America out of the wilderness and made it the greatest white country on earth."

Randy closes the film by thoughtfully explaining, "We're out there because the Civil War is coming. And the kids are going to have to be taught, because we're the future Klan."

Marysa stops the tape and hits "rewind" while Angela turns on the lights. "Why don't people arrest the KKK?," Alison immediately asks. "They're protected by the First Amendment," Marysa replies. "Also in a small town like that, people aren't going to stand up to it 'cause they'll probably believe it!," comments Alan. "They can pass out literature and wear their robes," Marlene adds, "but until they kill someone, or get caught killing someone, you can't do anything." Nora contributes: "I understand that they're protected by the First Amendment, but I also think that they might abuse it. You never know how far they'll go."

Acknowledging that there's a big controversy about this, Marysa mentions the case in which members of the American Nazi Party won the right to march in Skokie, Illinois, after having been defended by the ACLU on the grounds of freedom of speech. The proud son of a prominent civil liberties attorney, Josh corrects Marysa matter-of-factly: "Freedom to assemble." Marysa continues, putting forth the traditional civil liberties argument: "If you stop them, who decides the next group that cannot speak?" Abby and Marysa debate this point.

Abby: I think society should be able to decide who should not speak.

Marysa: But "society" can fluctuate from time to time, group to group.

Abby: But the majority of society is not in support of oppression.

Marysa: What about people under Hitler?

Abby: If Hitler hadn't had the right to free speech, people wouldn't have believed him!

Marysa: Where do you draw the line? How do you decide who can and who can't speak? The First Amendment protects everybody's rights.

Abby: But millions of people don't agree with them!

Marysa: Let's say we wouldn't let socialists or communists speak.

Abby: But they're not oppressing other people!

Marysa: Capitalists feel they are.

Abby: (Laughing) Well, they're wrong!

Marysa: Abby, there's a bit of tunnel vision here that we have to speak about. You can't just say that the only ones who can speak are those who agree with your position!

As in the case of the two earlier classes described, this resource film and the discussion that followed it raise the dilemma of how a democratic community that values free speech, diversity, and the open exchange of ideas can fairly address unpopular, controversial, or "wrong" points of view. Should those who voice these views be silenced, as Abby believes with regard to the KKK and to others who hold "oppressive" beliefs? And as Marysa—the individual holding the most power within the class—rejoins, who should define what constitutes "oppressive" and be empowered to enact this silencing? As we have seen, answers to these questions are no easier to find in the microcosm of the classroom than they are in Skokie, Illinois. Students' experience of these tensions is itself contradictory. On the one hand, they talk about valuing open-mindedness, a plurality of opinions, and the importance of free expression; on the other hand, at times they seek closure to controversies and rest easier in being told which opinions are "right."

For example, Sandra pays Steve a high compliment consistent

with her valuation of "keeping an open mind." "You know, Steve doesn't just read one book and say, well, this one book is right," she tells me during our interview. "He's the kind of person who reads lots of things, in depth." She criticizes Abby, by contrast, for failing to do the same: "Abby, she's not having an open mind! She's just so set about what she wants to believe. Abby's mom is a communist, and she teaches Abby things and Abby just always thinks, you know, my mom is always right."

But while Sandra values open-mindedness in theory, she herself finds it difficult to sustain. Overwhelmed by the diversity of opinions offered on the Middle East, she asks me to provide closure to this contentious debate. She explains:

> I don't know much about it, and I already told you that. Josh thinks it's fifty-fifty, that both people have their ancestors there, so it's both equally theirs. And that's all right, 'cause that's how I feel, too. But then there's that issue about how the people were moved out. And Abby says some of the same things that were used in the Holocaust were used there, like, murdering people, and some women were raped. And then Steve said that they were asked to leave, and they left voluntarily. So I don't know which to believe! Because Abby said she's read it in books, and that Steve just learned it in conservative books, and, see, I don't know! So who is more, who is more right?

In this instance and others, my answer to Sandra is nuanced and complex: as best I can, I try to give a historical account that takes into consideration both sides of the argument. But Sandra seems impatient with my refusal to choose sides. Furious with Abby for ideologically pressuring her, she jumps on my answers that qualify Abby's claims and ignores similar remarks that question Steve's perspective. For example, after a long exchange in which I have argued that I believe many Palestinians were, in fact, compelled to leave their land, I add, "What is absolutely *not* accurate is that millions of people were massacred—" and am interrupted by Sandra, who vehemently exclaims, "See! That's what [Abby] says!"

Disquieted by my refusal to grant either side full legitimacy, she eventually consoles herself in the best pluralist tradition: "There could be Steve's point of view, and [Abby's] point of view, and then mix them together and there could be something that they could come to."

Josh's approach to the problem is negotiated differently. At first glance, he seems to want to silence those with whom he disagrees. He argues for "killing" people who hold beliefs like those of Holocaust revisionist Jim Keegstra. He appears equally dismissive of Abby's point of view and seems not in the least compelled to address her claim. "It's not even really that true!" he tells me during our interview. "It's how things worked out! That the United Nations screwed up and put everyone in a small space and you have that problem. I think this country did the worse thing. This country had options. This country didn't have to kill all the Indians that were here, but they did. In Israel you have a problem! Everyone wants to kill each other. Even today."

A longtime friend of Chi-Ho's, however, Josh struggles with how not to dismiss his friend while at the same time dismissing his point of view. He feels torn between an impulse to shut Chi-Ho out altogether (as manifested in his desire to move his seat) and an impulse to engage him in struggle (as manifested in his ribbing of Chi-Ho in class). He ultimately supports the second position, though he clearly has difficulty doing so. Evoking the words of his much-revered father, Josh says, "I've been taught that you do not start violence with people, and that the only way to prove yourself as a great person is to talk to people, to make them see that what they're saying is so wrong, he said that. This is what me and my father used to disagree on, but I'm beginning to believe him."

Abby seems to embody most dramatically the tensions between valuing open-mindedness and taking a clear moral stance. Reflecting the political priorities of her parents, she argues passionately in favor of social change and sees eliciting different points of view as essential to achieving it: "I really believe that there needs to be some change in the world today! And I think a really impor-

tant part of change is understanding what someone else is thinking. To change other people, you really have to know what their
thought processes are, and what they think about." Having watched
her parents contend with different viewpoints in meetings and
demonstrations, she holds that it is important not only to know
what "goes on in other peoples' minds" but to relate to them
accordingly: "In talking to someone else, [my parents] might be
arguing or whatever, but they really try to understand what the
other person is thinking, and try to think of different ways they can
say things that they might understand, or that might change their
view. . . . Because if you just come out say what you think, and give
no regard to what the other person is thinking, then that will create
anger. And resentment. And they won't really be open to change."

Transposing her parents' world into her own, she explains how
important it is that a full range of views are expressed in the classroom, claiming that this is why she speaks up in class: "I think that
things have to be said! And maybe other people aren't as coura-
geous to say it, or they don't feel that they can say it, but somebody
has to say it at one point or another. Even if no one else in the room
is thinking what I have to say, there are still different points that
need to come out, and if someone says them, then it's
good. . . . 'Cause it's good to think about all points in any problem
or situation that may come up." Knowing the points of view of her
fellow classmates is important in this regard: "I'm usually one of the
only ones who is really speaking up, and I really want to know what
other people think about what I'm saying . . . so maybe I could
either argue it out, and really try to tell them what my point of view
was, or just hear what other people are thinking about. . . . Because
if they don't speak, I'm totally, totally closed off from anything that
they're thinking about."

But while Abby campaigns eloquently for lively debates in
which multiple points of view are brought out into the open, she
argues equally well against granting each view legitimacy. Far from
falling into a relativist trap, she asserts: "I do believe that there is
always a right thing! And a lot of people have the impression that

it's just your opinion? And your point of view? And they don't really give a chance to have one be right? It's just always 'your opinion,' or 'They should be able to say that because that's their opinion.' And I really, really don't agree with that!" Directly challenging the civil libertarian line promoted by Marysa in reference to the KKK, she charges: "A lot of people said, '[The KKK] should be able to have the freedom to speak because that's in the Constitution.' Well, if it's gonna hurt someone else then it shouldn't be there! That kind of idea should not be allowed to be promoted in any way because it's oppressive! I think that the right thing should always be promoted and the people who think otherwise should not be allowed to speak!" Entirely certain that the majority of the people in the country are against oppression, Abby suggests that this majority should be empowered to silence oppressive minority opinions. "If those oppressive ideas weren't being promoted all the time because of freedom of speech, the country would be a better place!"

Listening to Abby, I cannot help but realize that the majority she so fully trusts would probably suppress not only the Ku Klux Klan but also her Maoist parents. No doubt this is the point Marysa was getting at when she countered Abby's recommendation for "majority control" with the remark, "Let's say we wouldn't let socialists or communists speak." Aware that Marysa's broader point is lost on Abby, I ask how she reconciles the importance of articulating "different points of view" with the notion that some "should not be allowed to speak." She laughs a bit, pauses, starts to explain, stops, begins again, stops again, and then resumes in a voice softer than usual:

> I don't know. I mean I know what I'm trying to say in both situations, but I don't know how they go along with each other. I mean, in a discussion about something that's happening, like the Ku Klux Klan and their ideas, that's really a point of view, and what in my first statement I was talking about were situations that are happening in the world, or with other people. And that's not really a situation, what they preach, it's an idea. And if an idea actually is carried

out through to action that's oppressive, then that shouldn't be allowed to be expressed. But if you're talking about a situation in which something happened then it's good to bring out all points of it, 'cause, most of those situations are problems, and they need to be solved, and to solve a problem you have to know exactly what's happening in it from all perspectives! Do you understand?

In truth, I find it a bit difficult to follow Abby's train of thought, but I am mightily impressed by what she struggles to make clear to me. Abby is a thirteen-year-old girl, and here she shows herself to be a moral philosopher as well, grappling with issues that much older moral philosophers and other members of civil society have struggled with for a long time. The tension between freedom and constraint is at issue in Abby's deliberations; it is manifest in her conflict between valuing diversity, on the one hand, and condoning the censoring of oppressive viewpoints, on the other.

Though I believe most Americans would part company with Abby by at least paying lip service to traditional civil liberties arguments, many are uneasy about doing so. Tensions necessarily exist between the value of freedom of expression and the reality of having to defend the expression of beliefs some perceive to be harmful or repressive. Such tensions fueled the controversy over the ACLU's defense of the American Nazi Party's right to march in Skokie, Illinois, in 1977, and they fuel more recent debates about how American society should respond to the resurgence of neofascist groups that articulate (and sometimes act on) hateful attitudes toward homosexuals, Jews, persons of color, and other "subordinate" groups. Moreover, conflicts like these are not isolated to the United States. The alarming rise of neofascist groups in Germany, for example, has generated debate within that society about whether the government should limit or ban the expression of dangerously racist beliefs that have, of course, an eerily familiar ring.

The fury over "hate speech" codes on American college campuses, and the concern that these educational institutions increasingly allow only "politically correct" sentiments to be voiced, indicate that similar conflicts are alive and well in the educational arena. Tensions between students and teachers in Marysa's middle school classroom make clear that these conflicts exist at all levels of the educational domain.

Marysa was no doubt entirely sincere when she upheld diversity of political perspective as a strength to her students. "The diversity around you here, and the strengths from the differences of opinion you hear, and the strengths of the educational system you're in, encourage you to question and to learn different points of view," she noted positively by way of contrasting her own students' experience with that of the Klan youth. But many of Marysa's students were uncomfortable when they were confronted with the tension between valuing multiple perspectives and wanting perspectives they disagreed with to be silenced. Facing History's own teachers found this road difficult to negotiate as well. These findings show us just how dicey the "strength" of diversity can be.

This is why the tension between plurality and unity has been a focal point of debate throughout much of American history, and why it has also been key to American educational discourse. In recent years, these tensions have frequently surfaced in discussions over the merits or dangers of "values education" programs, most broadly defined. Conflicts arising from these tensions have been fought out in public forums ranging from local school boards to the federal government. But the tensions illuminated by these battles have a longer history, for they surface in educational debates that stretch back at least several decades.

We turn now to an examination of these historical and contemporary debates, examining both their theoretical underpinnings (Chapter Five), and their policy implications (Chapter Six). To understand them fully, however, we need to remember how they have played out in actual schools with actual children. For the issues these debates revolve around are not merely abstract; they affect students' experience in the classroom, even if they often ignore what goes on there, and what students themselves want and need.

Part Two

Public Debates

Chapter Five

Visions in Conflict

In August 1987, toward the middle of Ronald Reagan's second term in office, Phyllis Schlafly wrote an urgent letter to William Kristol, then chief of staff at the U.S. Department of Education. Schlafly—whose organizing career had begun with Barry Goldwater's 1964 presidential campaign—was a longtime leader of New Right causes. Her letter to Kristol was written on the letterhead of the Eagle Forum, an organization she had founded and headed that described itself as "leading the pro-family movement since 1972." In language both passionate and insistent, Schlafly denounced the Facing History and Ourselves program, claiming that its "psychological manipulation, induced behavioral change, and privacy-invading treatment are unacceptable in federally-funded or federally-approved curricula."

Among other things, Schlafly charged the program with violating the 1978 "Protection of Pupil Rights" statute, dubbed the "Hatch amendment" for its chief sponsor, conservative Utah Senator Orrin Hatch. This statute, for which no implementing federal regulations had ever been issued, prohibited schools from requiring students to undergo potentially revealing psychiatric or psychological testing or treatment without prior parental approval. Schlafly felt that by engaging students in discussion of moral and ethical issues and by having them record their private thoughts and feelings in journals, the Facing History program breached the spirit of the statute. "Americans do not appreciate having their children treated like guinea pigs in the classroom," she told Kristol. "I believe it would be most unfortunate if schools across the nation are permitted to believe that the Federal Government is sponsoring such a manipulative course in the public schools. Let's get back to 'basic skills' and 'what works.' "

Schlafly's letter to Kristol was not an isolated attack. She had in fact been lambasting the Facing History program since the early 1980s, in the *Schlafly Report*—the Eagle Forum's newsletter—as well as in public hearings conducted by the U.S. Department of Education in March 1984. As we will see in the next chapter, the charges leveled by Schlafly and her administration colleagues touched off a major controversy in educational policy-making that ultimately involved members of Congress, federal officials, the press, and parents, teachers, and students around the nation. This controversy concerned much more than the fate of a single curriculum, for by targeting FHAO, Schlafly gave herself a platform for addressing broader political issues: the fundamental rights of parents and students, the purpose of education in a democracy, and the nature of democracy itself.

The Fight Over Values in the Classroom

That these issues were fought out in the realm of education is not surprising, and that they took shape in conflicts over a particular curriculum is not without precedent. Over the years, numerous attempts have been made to reckon with the place of social and moral values in the classroom. Whether approached as an explicit subject of the curriculum or embedded in the everyday dealings of students and teachers, American schools have long sought to nurture students' ability to know right from wrong, to care about their classmates and caretakers and to treat them with respect, in short, to engage with the world by seeing themselves as responsible citizens, members of the human community. These teachings have always been hotly contested, for liberals and conservatives have often been in conflict over the place moral education should occupy within the school curriculum, which values schools should teach, and how they should do so.

Advocates of making moral education an explicit part of the curriculum have argued that it is the school's responsibility—alongside that of parents and other social and/or religious institutions—to teach children to become responsible and active citizens. Among other things, "responsibility" entails having some critical understanding of one's own beliefs and actions; some recognition that others may believe or act differently; and some framework for operating in ways that are neither harmful nor repressive (to oneself or to others) but that are, instead, conducive to resolving conflicts between others' actions and beliefs and one's own. In the increasingly ethnically and racially diverse American context, the values associated with such a definition of responsibility might include respect for cultural diversity and a commitment to safeguarding it. In this context, for example, teachers might object to students voicing racist or homophobic attitudes in the classroom, and they might work to create a climate critical of such attitudes.

Of course, supporters of addressing moral learning within the classroom do not see this as the school's sole (or even necessarily primary) agenda. They embrace the school's function of fostering cognitive growth and command of given content areas. They see moral learning as a parallel endeavor, at the very least, and as an element that may facilitate cognitive growth in other areas, more ambitiously. When moral learning is conceived in this way, proponents regard their endeavor as critical to democracy.

Opponents of this kind of moral education in the classroom are by no means against responsible citizenship, and many would object to a characterization that pits them against the ideals of cultural tolerance and respect. They are a diverse group, and their reasons for opposing such curricula are consequently varied. Generally speaking, however, critics argue that moral values are by and large a private affair outside the purview of government. They feel that the responsibility for promoting moral growth lies with the home or the church, not the school. Moreover, they fear that the values promoted within the classroom may at times conflict with those encouraged at home. Equally invested in advancing a particular understanding of American democracy, they contest the so-called liberal biases of these educational programs and charge that they undermine, rather than further, democratic aims. Fearing the construction of values promoted by liberals within the schools and hoping to maintain control of children's moral education, critics argue against shared responsibility for moral growth. They urge schools to stick to a more limited intellectual terrain instead—for example, the old "basics" of reading, writing, and arithmetic.

These divergent attitudes toward what schools are (or should be) doing, attitudes underpinned by conflicting visions of the purpose and methods of public education in this country, have surfaced in many different arenas: in national political debates; in educational policy-making circles on the state and federal level; and in local battles over which courses should be taught, which textbooks should be purchased and assigned, and which pedagogical methods should be used.

As one in a long list of curricula attempting to instill moral values in American youth, the Facing History and Ourselves program itself became the subject of a heated public controversy in the mid 1980s and early 1990s. This controversy illustrates how interactions among citizens groups, the media, and policy makers influenced educational policy-making, funding, and public perceptions of key issues in American schooling. But to make sense of the battle over Facing History, we need to situate the arguments of both the program's advocates and its critics in the context of broader historical debates over education, and over social and cultural issues more generally. Education has long been seen as central to shaping our identity as a nation. Political conflicts over the character of American society and its future direction are therefore often manifested in debates over the purpose, content, and methods of American public schooling, while debates about education often raise more broadly contentious issues.

So although the controversy that involved Facing History and Ourselves had many distinctive aspects and unfolded within a specific political context, it was prefigured by earlier battles over controversial curricula. Moreover, the contours of this particular controversy were in important ways shaped by the character and outcomes of previous struggles over the goals and methods of public education, and therefore over the definition of American society and the meaning of American democracy.

These struggles go back at least a century, though one could trace their origins to the founding of the American republic, since moral education, in one form or another, has always been a part of America's educational mission. The discussion that follows will focus more specifically on theorists and approaches most directly relevant to understanding the Facing History program and the controversy in which it became engulfed.

Learning Through Doing: John Dewey and the Progressive Education Movement

An excellent point of departure for understanding educational debates over much of the past century is the work of philosopher and educator John Dewey (1859–1952). Dewey's educational theories and curricular innovations ushered in profound changes in American schooling, which were controversial in his own time and continue to be today. Placing itself squarely within the Dewey legacy, Facing History has, not surprisingly, been subject to some of the same criticisms Dewey's work has been subjected to since the early 1900s.

Like others in the Progressive Era, Dewey was cognizant of enormous changes taking place in American society due to large-scale immigration, rapid industrialization, and urbanization. He accepted his period's faith in scientific progress and the need for purposeful intervention to "fix" society's problems. Melding the relatively new study of child psychology with the older, Rousseauean notion of a child's nature and potential, Dewey looked to the school as an instrument for redressing social inequity. In so doing, he challenged the prevailing consensus embodied in the 1893 *Committee of Ten Report*—that education "should be directed toward training the powers of observation, memory, expression, and reasoning"—and instead embraced the educational objectives later articulated by the 1918 *Cardinal Principles of Secondary Education* ("health, command of fundamental processes, worthy home-membership, vocation, citizenship, worthy use of leisure, and ethical character").[1]

Dewey rejected the notion that knowledge exists "out there," in facts to be accumulated and memorized by the passive learner. Instead, he cast the student as a powerful creator of knowledge who learned through *doing*, through the directed integration of personal experience and so-called objective realities, and through the continual process of critical inquiry and reflection. He put forward a theory of moral development that rested on the child's ability to think critically and reflectively rather than on his or her absorption of moral lessons (be they religious or secular in tone) handed down throughout the school day. He saw schools as "communities" of learners, as agencies of individuals bent on changing their habits and their minds so as to change and reconstruct society itself. Dewey's theory of education profoundly influenced school practice from his own time until today. His conception of the school as an organ of social mobility and equity, and not simply a conduit of knowledge; his reliance on psychology for designing a child-centered, differentiated, and student-empowering curriculum; and his construction of education as a profoundly democratic and moral activity have informed not only the pedagogy of Facing History and Ourselves and other values-oriented curricula, but also that of programs less self-consciously concerned with promoting social responsibility. One could argue that mainstream pedagogy in the United States is largely shaped by some interpretation of Dewey's principles.

Dewey has been criticized from the Left for his naive faith in scientific progress and for his apparent belief that schools could redress social inequity without directly confronting social, political, and economic problems. But, over the years, Dewey and others in the Progressive education movement have been criticized much more virulently by conservative critics. The passion behind these attacks speaks to the enormousness of the changes Dewey and other Progressive educators brought about.

Teaching the "American Problem": The Controversy Over the Rugg Social Studies Texts

A noteworthy example can be seen in the late 1930s and early 1940s, when vehement opposition was aroused in response to a series of social studies textbooks written by progressive educator Harold Rugg. "Books on civics and social science have split this little western Ohio town wide open in a row over the teaching of Communism," an April 9, 1940, article in the *Cleveland Press* reported. "The rural Red hunt . . . has resulted in . . . the burning of a fiery cross in front of the home of the . . . school board president . . . [and the] dramatic burning of a dozen library schoolbooks in the school furnace."[2]

Just what were these dangerous books? Between 1923 and 1926, Harold Rugg, a professor of education at Teachers College of Columbia University, wrote a series of "experimental pamphlets" on the social sciences for use in middle school grades. The pamphlets were adopted for trial use by several hundred school systems in nearly forty states; after considerable revision and expansion, they were published commercially by Ginn and Co. in 1929. The "Man and His Changing Society" series eventually included twenty textbooks for use by students in primary through secondary school. By Rugg's own estimate, not less than five million students studied one or more of his texts over an eleven-year period.[3]

Rugg pioneered the field of "social studies"—a holistic and relational approach to teaching about American social life. His books integrated lessons from history, civics, geography, sociology, and economics—fields that had previously been approached as distinct and unrelated disciplines. A product of the Progressive education movement, Rugg believed firmly in a child-centered and social-minded curriculum. "Through the study of society and its problems the school must devote itself to the development of sensitive, clear-headed, fearless, and confident young men and women who understand American life as it is actually lived and are determined to make it a magnificent civilization for themselves and their children," he wrote in *That Men May Understand*, a 1941 book rebutting the charges of those who had attacked his textbooks. "To this end the life and program of the school must be designed directly from the culture of the people, not from a classics-entrenched curriculum. Now is the time to build not a subject-centered school but a truly society-centered as well as a child-centered one."[4]

To understand "American life as it is actually lived," Rugg felt that students needed to understand America's weaknesses as well as its strengths. Stressing education's importance in achieving and sustaining a truly democratic society, he felt students must grapple with the disparity between America's potential and its actuality—a gap he defined as the fundamental "American problem." Rugg argued that democracy in essence required youth to know the "full story—the deficiencies as well as the achievements of our society, the problems and issues as well as the narrative of adventure." His approach to history was informed by the work of the "New Historians"—academics like Charles A. Beard, Frederick J. Turner, James Harvey Robinson, and Albert Bushnell Hart, who had sought to replace earlier, usually laudatory accounts of America's past with more "objective," "scientific" assessments of the colonial period, the Revolution, the conflict over slavery, westward expansion, and so forth. In concert with this new breed, Rugg's texts often highlighted points of conflict in American society. In discussing the drafting of the Constitution, for example, he mentioned disparities between rich and poor, noting that the document's signatories were landowners and that the Constitution served their economic interests. In addressing contemporary society, he noted that while America had the highest standard of living in the world and was potentially "a land of plenty," it was, nevertheless, a severely depressed society in a state of economic crisis. He detailed shifts from private to public ownership throughout his texts (addressing arenas like water resources and schooling, for example), pointing to tensions that at times arose between public and private interests.[5]

In short, instead of shying away from a discussion of conflicts within American society, Rugg purposefully sought to induce students to confront them. True to the Progressive spirit, he did so by providing "a core of pupil activities, dynamic and thought-provoking." Workbooks accompanying each scholarly text "compelled" students to "find the answer to one or more important questions"; gone were the days of mere memorization or recitation. In defense of his approach, Rugg said, "It is my thesis that if we are to have consent in a democratic people it must be built upon the study of controversial issues, because such study is the intellectual foundation of the schools. One of the chief plans of my program is that the young people shall be urged constantly to *take thought before they take sides*, but it is obvious that to 'take thought' to make choices, they must confront the alternatives set out clearly before them. How else can human beings practice decision making than by confronting issues?"[6]

Denouncing his textbooks as communistic, anti-American, and dangerous, a group of businessmen and nativist organizations launched an all-out crusade against Rugg in 1939 and 1940. Leading the attack was a small group of business leaders, among them Bertie C. Forbes, a columnist for Hearst newspapers and the owner of *Forbes* magazine, and Merwin K. Hart, president of the New York State Economic Council and an advocate of cutting federal taxes as well as funding for public education. These men and others saw Rugg's attention to economic interpretations of American history as inherently subversive of faith in free enterprise. Newspapers in the Hearst chain trumpeted these allegations.

Conservative groups joined in the attack as well. Organizations like the Daughters of the American Revolution, the American Legion, and the Veterans of Foreign Wars objected to Rugg's desire to stimulate students' critical engagement with controversial American issues. Urging the textbooks' removal from Philadelphia schools, Mrs. Ellwood J. Turner, the corresponding secretary of the

Daughters of Colonial Wars, noted that Rugg "tried to give the child an unbiased viewpoint instead of teaching him real Americanism. . . . All the old histories taught my country, right or wrong. That's the point of view we want our children to adopt. We can't afford to teach them to be unbiased and let them make up their minds."[7] Magazines like *American Legion* and *Liberty* echoed these views, alerting parents to the growing danger. A September 1940 article published in *American Legion* was distributed to one million homes throughout the states. Entitled "Treason in the Textbooks," the piece charged that Rugg would soon convince students that the " 'capitalistic system' is the fault of selfish fellows like Benjamin Franklin and Thomas Jefferson who wanted to save their property; that the poor man wasn't given proper consideration; that in Russia the youth are engaged in creating a beautiful, new democratic order; . . . that advertising is an economic waste; [and] that morality is a relative value."[8]

The well-orchestrated attack against Rugg succeeded in fomenting conflict in communities across the country. In some instances, textbooks were in fact removed from schools. Though some communities no doubt agreed with critics' charges, others (like Binghamton, New York) simply agreed to remove the texts so as to avoid further controversy. Many teachers and students defended the "Man and His Changing Society" series, and some communities succeeded in keeping the books—most notably Englewood, New Jersey, where Forbes had served on the board of education and had first launched the anti-Rugg campaign. Whether the books went or stayed, however, the battle did damage far and wide by dividing local communities and arousing fear of censorship within the schools.

Education: The Battleground for America's Soul

Though the battle over Rugg was perhaps the most notable example of backlash, opposition to the pedagogical and subject-matter reforms of the Progressive educators continued for decades. As Peter

Dow has shown, the Cold War climate of the 1940s and 1950s provided the setting in which retired businessman Mortimer Smith and educator and scholar Bernard Iddings Bell again took the offensive.[9] Smith's 1949 *And Madly Teach* criticized the social goals of the Progressive education movement. Foreshadowing philosopher Allan Bloom's plea decades later, Smith urged schools to return to promoting a Platonic ideal of the "good." He also championed the school's potential for fostering "individual betterment" and rejected its role as an agent of "social solidarity." Bell's *Crisis in Education: A Challenge to American Complacency*, also published in 1949, urged a return to the traditional fare of liberal arts, humanistic studies, and religion. Both Bell and Smith criticized Progressive educational reforms for their pragmatism and scientific orientation and objected to their promotion of social goals in education.[10]

These attitudes were picked up by journalists, academics, and the public at large, becoming the subject of organizing campaigns by the 1960s. In 1962, for example, the electoral race for the position of California's state superintendent of public instruction won national attention when Max Rafferty, a respected educational leader, defeated the favored candidate by campaigning on an anti-Progressive plank. Rafferty won over parents who shared his belief that traditional subject matter and teaching methods were more effective avenues for learning than the experiential methods of the Progressives. Parents also shared Rafferty's concern that the Progressives focused too much on the school as an agency of social reform, and that their methods invited a host of undesirable outcomes—among them amoral behavior, relativist thinking, and favorable attitudes toward socialism and other forms of what they saw as anti-Americanism.[11]

These concerns were shared by a variety of groups on the Right, some of them veterans of the Goldwater campaign. In the late 1960s and early 1970s, former Goldwater activists like Richard Viguerie, Paul Weyrich, and Phyllis Schlafly began to pull together a coalition of groups that focused on social and cultural issues rather than simply free-market economics. These groups campaigned against abortion rights, the Equal Rights Amendment, Affirmative Action, gun control, foreign aid, and federal funding for social programs. Unlike the traditional, elitist conservative movement, the New Right was populist in tone and sought to build a mass base. Its secular leaders (like Richard Viguerie, whose pioneering work in direct-mail fundraising helped to found several New Right organizations) and its religious leaders (like televangelists Jerry Falwell and Pat Robertson) mobilized thousands across the country to become politically active crusaders for New Right causes.[12]

New Right members saw education as a vital battleground in the struggle for America's soul and joined conservative forces in organizing against the heirs of the Progressive legacy. For example, Superintendent Rafferty's charges were echoed by his contemporary John A. Stormer, an early leader in the Christian fundamentalist movement and an activist in Barry Goldwater's presidential campaign. In his 1964 seven-million-copy best-seller, *None Dare Care it Treason*, Stormer attacked the wide-scale revision of textbooks and teaching methods brought about by the Progressive education movement. He criticized Rugg's "Man and His Changing Society" texts in particular, saying that they "downgrad[ed] American heroes and the U.S. Constitution," had a pronounced "anti-religious bias," and were "propaganda for socialistic control of men's lives."[13] Stormer also charged that Rugg's mentor, John Dewey, "rejected fixed moral laws" and "adopted relativistic concepts as his guiding philosophy." In so doing, Stormer argued, Dewey believed that "teaching children any of the absolutes of morals, government, or ethics was a waste of time."[14]

Charges like these were repeated throughout the 1970s, 1980s, and 1990s, by both the secular and religious arms of the New Right. In fact, the contemporary conservative and New Right critique of American education is grounded in opposition to the schools' alleged promotion of an anti-American social agenda and to its encouragement of amoral relativism. Both problems are partially attributed to Dewey and to Progressive educators more generally, who are accused of having emphasized the child's critical meaning-making capacities rather than God-given absolutes.

The "Invisible Enemy": Values Clarification and Secular Humanism

In the mid 1960s and early 1970s, a new approach to moral education emerged that aroused the ire of educators across the political spectrum. Developed by university professors to provide hands-on teaching strategies for classroom practitioners, the "values clarification" method was influenced by Dewey in that its originators saw the classroom as an appropriate arena for addressing values and believed that children could make value decisions through undertaking a process of moral reasoning. However, the approach also departed from Dewey's in that it advanced individually determined values rather than socially conscious democratic ethics.

In fact, values clarification argued against promoting any particular set of values at all. It saw earlier approaches to moral education—like religious teachings or the *McGuffey Reader*, which had sought to instill in students a host of traditional (and secular) values like trustworthiness, thrift, and honesty—as both indoctrinating and ineffective in achieving their purpose. The goal of values clarification was not to get children to adopt a socially sanctioned sense of right and wrong, but to get them to determine their own sense of justice. According to its originators, this clarifying process helped children become aware of the consequences of their values and of other alternatives. It sought to instill in children a willingness to publicly affirm their values and to demonstrate commitment by acting on behalf of them. Because of the emphasis on process over content, teachers were warned against expressing judgment over values students voiced in class. Values teachers might well find repugnant (racism, support for shoplifting, advocacy of lying, and so forth) could be "neutrally" questioned but never criticized. Though teachers might, at times, express their own beliefs about a given subject, they were instructed to posit them as simply one belief among many. Privileging neither the authority of the teacher nor any other socially authoritative voice (such as that of parents or religious institutions), the approach argued that everyone is entitled to his or her values, as long as they have been critically examined (through free choice and the weighing of alternatives) and affirmed (through public acknowledgment and action).

Values clarification became extremely popular with practitioners in the late 1960s and early 1970s for a variety of reasons. By affirming the individual student's efforts to determine his or her own values and beliefs, the approach embodied certain premises of that socially transformative period—for example, an antiauthority ideal and the approbation of the individual's freedom from oppressive social constraints. The approach was also easy to implement, since it provided teachers with a panoply of simple, easily replicable exercises that could be carried out at any point in the school day. For these reasons, values clarification caught on like wildfire and was soon practiced in classrooms across the country.

Values clarification exercises typically involved brief exchanges between a teacher and students wherein a teacher would pose a simple value question (for example, "What is something you believe in?"), and then "promote clarity" by asking students to support their responses and to state whether they had, in fact, acted on behalf of the stated value. A variety of strategies were employed in which students might be asked to role-play, vote on ethical situations, make either-or choices, or rank various moral dilemmas.

Despite its popularity with practitioners, values clarification was vehemently attacked by educators on the Right but also by the Left. Many saw the approach as alarmingly relativistic; here sure-fire absolutes were replaced with what seemed like an extreme form of subjectivism. Since the approach encouraged clarity rather than the evaluation of moral content, values entirely antithetical to the public good (stealing, lying, treating others with disrespect, and so forth) might be voiced and implicitly validated. When University of Wisconsin assistant professor Alan L. Lockwood charged in the September 1975 issue of Teachers College Record that "values clarification embodies ethical relativism as its moral point of view," he reflected the concerns of many. "A program of value education which devotes its attention to questions of personal preference and desire presents a truncated and myopic view of morality. A program which avoids the controversies associated with value conflict, conflict resolution, and moral justification trivializes the complexity of value issues in human affairs," he said.[15]

Critics also argued that values clarification's claim to "neutrality" was false. Though instructed to contain his or her judgment, a teacher's questions of students were necessarily and inescapably value-bound.

Finally, conservative and New Right critics argued that the method valued certain humanist premises—individual autonomy, free choice, an antiauthoritarian notion of equality—which they regarded as extremely dangerous. They claimed that the Left was in fact indoctrinating children with their own religious faith—one that denied the belief in a transcendent God and instead placed human beings at the center of its concerns. The Right dubbed this new religion "secular humanism." They charged it with rejecting the belief in an immutable, definable right and wrong and embracing instead the values of pluralism and situational ethics, and the notion that there are multiple ways to understand reality. Linking the emergence of secular humanism with the teachings of Dewey, New Right critics charged that by rejecting absolute authority and values, the secular humanists undermined the sanctity of both home and nation. In this vein, adherents of "secular humanism" were accused of favoring communism and undermining the security of the United States. A 1968 book endorsed by Billy James Hargis of the Christian Crusade typically linked secular humanism with treachery.[16] As Chip Berlet and Margaret Quigley note in their article "Traditional Values, Racism, and Christian Theocracy: The Right-Wing Revolt Against the Modern Age," this book argued that "the liberal . . . would dissolve the American Republic and crush the American dream so that our nation and our people might become another faceless number in an internationalist state."[17]

From the critique against values clarification onward, "secular humanism" became the war cry in the New Right's battle against what it perceived as the liberal takeover of the schools. "It's time to expose the hypocrisy of those who have so dogmatically chased God and the Bible out of the public schools in the name of freedom of religion, and then forced their own Humanist religion on the children instead," Schlafly said in the June 1983 issue of her monthly *Report.* "Every time a teacher rejects or refuses to recognize God's moral law as codified in the Ten Commandments, and tells the child that we cannot or should not be judgmental about stealing, lying, killing, maiming, blaspheming, fornicating, or coveting, that teacher is teaching the religion of Humanism. Every time a teacher rejects or ridicules the notion that God created man and the earth, that teacher is teaching the religion of Humanism."[18]

Critics like the Heritage Foundation's Onalee McGraw charged that "humanistic education purports to train the young how to order their daily lives in terms of ethical decision-making and to develop their own autonomous value systems. In the humanistic frame of reference, however, values are relative and ethics are situational. Children are therefore being taught at school that moral and social beliefs and behavior are not necessarily based upon Judeo-Christian principles being taught by most families at home."[19] Or as fundamentalist Baptist preacher and Moral Majority leader Tim LaHaye succinctly put it in his 1980 *The Battle for the Mind,* "An invisible enemy threatens our society. Its name? Humanism. Its target? Your mind."[20] Some communities fought back against the "secular humanist" turn: in July 1976, for example, the board of education of Frederick County, Maryland, adopted a policy strictly prohibiting values clarification and other "secular humanist" approaches in their schools.[21]

But values clarification was also criticized from other perspectives. Divorced from the curriculum, the approach upheld values as entities unto themselves and failed to demonstrate that moral questions in fact underlie the lessons of history, literature, and all other subject matter. Attempting to nurture the student's autonomous moral compass, teachers often raised, queried, and dropped important moral issues within a matter of minutes, leaving students responsible for private moral reflection but giving them little guidance in how to go about it. Lacking a developmental focus, the method neglected to consider students' abilities and limits for engaging in moral reflection; it also mistakenly assumed their willingness to voice their opinions freely, indifferent to the approval or condemnation of their peers. And prizing the individual's quest for clarity above the potential for social community, the method allowed for divergent, often conflictual points of view to be raised in the classroom but failed to provide students with a means for reckoning with their differences.

Supporters of moral education generally commended values clarification's departure from the McGuffey Reader and other indoctrinating approaches. They particularly applauded its teachers' use of the Socratic "why?" Supporters also appreciated the method's insistence that moral action must accompany moral belief. But because of the shortcomings cited above, many also looked for alternative approaches to engendering critical moral reflection in the schools.

Fostering Moral Dialogue in the Classroom: Lawrence Kohlberg and the Developmentalists

In the mid 1970s, developmental psychologist Lawrence Kohlberg and his colleagues offered an alternative to values clarification by positing that a child's moral growth takes place by moving through a series of distinct and universal stages of moral reasoning rather than by attaining increased awareness of individually held beliefs. From longitudinal studies conducted with boys around the globe over a period of twenty-odd years, Kohlberg concluded that there was a hierarchy of six stages of ethical thought, marked by an individual's progression from pragmatic, personal considerations to an increasing ability to understand another's perspective, integrate conflicting points of view, and embrace and act on universal ethical principles. Kohlberg's stages were considered "developmental" in that one's reasoning at higher moral stages necessarily incorporated one's understanding at lower ones. He consequently argued that the goal of moral education was to help children progress from one stage to another.

This clearly delineated telos distinguished Kohlberg's approach from the moral relativity and personalism of values clarification, while sharing that model's rejection of indoctrinating methods and its use of the Socratic "why?" approach. At the heart of Kohlberg's theory was the notion that the aim of education should be cognitive and affective development, not simply the intellectual mastery of subject matter. This notion was inspired by Dewey's earlier argument: "The aim of education is growth or development both intellectual and moral. . . . Ethical and psychological principles can aid the school in the greatest of all constructions—the building of a free and powerful character. Only knowledge of the order and connection of the stages in psychological development can insure this. Education is the work of supplying the conditions which will enable the psychological functions to mature in the freest and fullest manner."[22]

Kohlberg also drew on the work of developmental psychologist Jean Piaget in defining the structure of moral reasoning. Piaget had applied Dewey's developmental theory to his work with children in the late 1930s and 1940s, arguing that all individuals move through invariant stages of logical reasoning as they mature—from the child's initial ability to reason only about concrete data (the so-called "concrete operational" stage) to his or her ability to reason abstractly (the "formal operational" stage, which is usually a hallmark of adolescence). Kohlberg's moral sequence was tied to Piaget's finding that logical maturation marks a move from the concrete to the abstract.

The values of liberty, equality, and reciprocity were central to Kohlberg's moral schema. His ideas were consequently informed by the liberal tradition's claim that moral judgments are made in adherence to principles of justice that are universally applicable to all of humankind. Since progress through moral stages is manifested in one's increasing attendance to these allegedly universal concerns, Kohlberg—like Dewey before him—envisioned moral education as a profoundly civic activity, crucial to the perpetuation of democracy.

What could schools do to catalyze this essential development? Kohlberg and his colleagues proposed reforms in both curriculum and school governance. Chief among them was their advocacy of purposeful moral dialogue within the classroom, involving students' discussion of hypothetical or real-life moral dilemmas that posed compelling alternatives based on conflicting moral claims. In classrooms across the country, students debated a variety of actions protagonists could take in response to a moral dilemma and justified their reasoning for choosing certain actions over others.

This emphasis on moral dialogue grew out of the research findings of Kohlberg and his then–doctoral student Moshe Blatt. Earlier, Kohlberg had argued that the transition from lower to higher stages of moral reasoning occurs when an individual's customary, stage-level beliefs are challenged by an unsettling situation of moral conflict. He had likewise claimed that individuals understand moral issues at their own stage, at all stages beneath their own, and at one stage above it. Finally, he had argued that in attempting to resolve moral conflicts, they naturally seek out the highest, most complex reasoning they can grasp. Building on Kolhberg's findings, Blatt called for purposefully introducing situations of moral conflict into the classroom and for bringing students of varying stages of moral development together to discuss them. By triggering moral conflicts (within individuals and within their classroom community) and by mixing students of varying moral stages, "lower"-stage thinkers would be motivated to sort through moral conflicts and would be helped in doing so by individuals at contiguous, higher stages of reasoning.

Teachers committed to moral education adopted Kohlberg and Blatt's schema and introduced moral dilemmas for discussion, typically within the framework of social studies and/or English classes.

The dilemmas they used for moral discussion were usually hypothetical (such as the well-known case where a poor man named "Heinz" is forced to choose between stealing a drug to save his dying wife or letting her die because he lacks the money to buy the drug), but at times they were culled from students' actual history lessons. Whether real or hypothetical, moral dilemma discussions were characterized by heterogeneously grouping students and encouraging them to voice their opinions freely. These discussions focused on moral reasoning (why Heinz should or should not steal the drug) rather than promoting the "right" moral action; teachers used the Socratic "why?" method to kindle students' reasoning at higher moral stages.

But Kohlberg claimed that the moral atmosphere of the entire school influenced a student's moral potential, and thus he eventually looked beyond the microcosm of the classroom to stimulate development. In select locales across the country (Cambridge and Brookline, Massachusetts; Scarsdale, New York; Pittsburgh, Pennsylvania), he set about establishing school governance structures based on participatory democracy. These "Just Community Schools" engaged students and teachers alike in discussions about school discipline, punishment, reward structures, and so forth. Through debating real-life dilemmas in class and community meetings, all members of a school community were to be responsible for establishing a moral environment characterized by fairness, reciprocity, and respect.

Though Kohlberg's cognitive-developmental theory and in-school practice avoided many of the pitfalls of the values clarification approach, it, too, had its share of critics. Some argued that neither his moral stages nor his ethical principles were in fact universal. For example, psychologist Carol Gilligan took issue with Kohlberg's all-male sample and with data indicating that girls scored lower on his developmental scale. She posited instead that individuals speak in two moral "voices"—the one Kohlberg identified, attuned to issues of equality and justice (generally favored by males), and another she herself identified, attuned to issues of care and attachment (generally favored by females). Building on Kohlberg's construct but finding it partial and gender biased, Gilligan offered a more holistic and integrative way to think about identifying and supporting moral growth.

Other critics complained that Kohlberg demanded too much of teachers; they felt that facilitating moral discussions within the classroom was simply not practicable. Still others questioned whether discussions of moral dilemmas were as beneficial as they had been touted to be.

Not surprisingly, Kohlberg was also heavily criticized by the New Right. In her 1976 pamphlet *Secular Humanism and the Schools: The Issue Whose Time Has Come*, Heritage Foundation consultant Onalee McGraw charged that Kohlberg's theory "holds to the same humanistic tenets—that is, the view that man is autonomous and pragmatically oriented" as values clarification did before it. Commending Kohlberg's approach for its rejection of moral relativism, she nonetheless attacked it for being "based on materialistic values found and affirmed by humanists without regard for the Judeo-Christian moral order, which is based upon the existence and fatherhood of a personal God."[23]

New Right activist Barbara Morris went one step further when she charged in her 1979 pamphlet, *Change Agents in the Schools: Destroy Your Children, Betray Your Country*, that Kohlberg's goal of stimulating students' moral growth was an attempt to subvert parental values. She also took issue with Kohlberg's methods in the classroom, finding his deliberate attempt to "upset the equilibrium of the child by setting up a situation where he experiences sufficient conflict in solving a problem" to be psychologically harmful. Finally, Morris objected to Kohlberg's conception of development itself, finding fault with his belief that one's adherence to transcendent ethical principles represented a higher stage of moral development than obedience to the strictures of state or religion. Like other critics on the Right, she feared that Kohlberg's schema would undermine social cohesion by promoting social anarchy rather than moral growth.[24]

Grappling with Difference: Multiculturalism, Antiracism, and Conflict Resolution

From the 1970s onward, the battle over conflicting educational visions took on new dimensions with the emergence of the issue of multiculturalism. Educators influenced by both the civil rights movement and the new focus on ethnic politics began to pay increasing attention to how the diversity of American society should be understood and characterized to schoolchildren. The metaphor of America as a "melting pot" where ethnic differences would ultimately disappear, subsumed within a new, more or less homogeneous and distinctively "American" identity, began to lose ground. Instead, some turned to a new vision of "cultural pluralism," according to which ethnic and racial groups would retain (and even enhance) their distinctive identities while coexisting in an atmosphere of mutual tolerance and respect for diversity. Responsive to this trend, and partially responsible for the momentum behind it, many educators sought to instill in their students a respect for cultural diversity.

Though calls for paying more attention to the contributions of non-Western cultures were heard in the late 1960s and early 1970s, they were not central issues in curricular reform until the 1980s. As described by *Education Week*, arguably the nation's chief chronicle of educational concerns, earlier efforts to promote multicultural awareness were often simply added on to the already established curriculum, set aside in elective courses, or relegated to specific periods of the year, such as "Black History Month." Advocates of a more thorough and integrative approach considered these earlier attempts woefully superficial—James Banks, a University of Washington multicultural educator, called it a "tepees and chitlins" strategy. Provoked in part by demographic shifts within U.S. society (by the year 2000, for example, 46 percent of the nation's schoolchildren will be nonwhite), multicultural initiatives moved to a more central place in the curriculum in the 1980s, accompanied by heated debate.[25]

Advocates of multiculturalism are a diverse group, and the movement has meant different things to different people. At the risk of generalizing, multiculturalism at its core promotes a set of interrelated values: an increased understanding and affirmation of one's own cultural heritage; a recognition of cultural diversity, coupled with a valuation of diversity itself; a heightened interest in learning about other cultures, as well as a genuine respect for cultures different from one's own. Like the curricular initiatives already described, multiculturalism's proponents see its values as conducive to students' intellectual growth and to their active participation in a democratic polity.

Within this general framework, multicultural advocates lay stress on different elements. Building on multicultural values but going beyond the mere acknowledgment and appreciation of difference, programs in antiracism actively promote the belief that all races and peoples are equal. These programs seek to cultivate in children an awareness of inequities in power and economic status, as well as knowledge of how social and legal institutions have addressed the problem of race relations. At times, antiracism programs team up with initiatives in conflict resolution, where students are taught to reflect critically on the differences that divide them (be they based in race, gender, class, religion, or sexuality) and are trained to mediate conflicts among members of their school community.

Courses in "ethnic studies" (African-American, Native American, and so forth) offer another approach. Often targeting children of color, they seek to redress the notion of cultural deficiency by teaching about the histories and contributions of people of color and in so doing help to strengthen students' self-esteem. Cities with model programs include Portland, Oregon, where since 1989 essays on the contributions of Africans and African Americans have been integrated throughout the curriculum in six different fields of study, and Milwaukee, Wisconsin, which in 1990 voted to establish two "African-American immersion" schools exclusively for black males, featuring an Afrocentric curriculum.

Not surprisingly, these varied initiatives have garnered both support and criticism on intellectual, psychological, and social grounds.
Supporters contend that the historical perspective provided by multiculturalism is richer and more complete than the overwhelmingly
white, Eurocentric focus that dominates much of traditional school
learning. They also contend that these programs are vital to the
empowerment of children of color and useful in cultivating and sustaining their interest in school. Finally, they argue multiculturalism's merits on the grounds of the increasing diversity of American
society. By teaching all children about the contributions of the
diverse peoples that comprise the American populace, they argue,
children of all races and ethnic groups will become more knowl-
edgeable, understanding, and respectful of the variety of individuals with whom they will interact in their lives.

Throughout the 1980s and into the early 1990s, the supporters
of these claims butted up against the Reagan and Bush administrations' concerns about the apparent failures of the American school
system, and more precisely against their call for a return to curricular "basics." Both Republican administrations blamed renewed
attention to the school's social role for the perceived decline in
"educational excellence" signaled by dropping SAT scores and students' poor performance in mathematics, literacy skills, and other
areas. Thus charges issued against Dewey and other Progressive educators in the 1930s and 1940s have resurfaced in today's multicultural debates.

Critics of multiculturalism also charge that it at times goes too
far, sacrificing historical accuracy in the interest of including
minority groups and slighting fundamental subject matter in the
interest of altering the traditional bill of fare. They also charge it
with fracturing social cohesion in the interest of proclaiming diversity. And perhaps most disturbing, they contend that it promotes
new forms of racial intolerance in the interest of fostering appreciation of people of color. In New York State, for example, a controversy erupted in 1990 when the board of regents authorized the
revision of the state's public school curriculum along multicultural

lines. A draft of the report urging curricular reform came under fire
from various directions. Critics included a group of noted historians, among them Arthur Schlesinger, Jr. (author of many books on
American history and politics, including *The Age of Jackson* and
The Disuniting of America), and Diane Ravitch (at that time an
adjunct professor of history and education at Columbia University's
Teachers College, and from 1991 to 1993 Assistant Secretary of
Education at the U.S. Department of Education). Although these
historians pledged their commitment to equal rights and a "pluralistic interpretation of American history," they also charged that
the report showed "no understanding of the integrity of history as
an intellectual discipline" but instead "saw history . . . as a form of
social and psychological therapy whose function is to raise the self-
esteem of children from minority groups." The historians con-
demned the report's denigration of Western culture and its
"reduction of history to ethnic cheerleading." "Little can have
more damaging effect on the republic than the use of the school
system to promote the division of our people into antagonistic
racial groups," they said.[26]

Many in the New Right link multiculturalism with the plethora
of ills associated with humanism. As Chip Berlet and Margaret
Quigley point out, these critics see multiculturalism as simply a new
form of relativism, one implicitly hostile to America's democratic
heritage. For example, New Right critic Samuel Blumenfeld decries
the movement for affirming diverse life-styles and value systems,
thereby implicitly legitimizing a moral diversity that "directly con-
tradicts the Biblical concept of moral absolutes on which this
nation was founded." In the absence of "inculcat[ing] a common set
of moral and spiritual values based on our Judeo-Christian heritage,"
Blumenfeld argues, the American public school has become nothing more than "a marketplace for competing pagan and anti-
Christian systems." He contends that "it is now official policy of the
government schools to deny that there exists a common value system known as Americanism—unless by Americanism you mean
moral anarchy."[27]

Still others within the radical Right oppose multiculturalism on racial nativist grounds. For example, former presidential candidate Patrick Buchanan links multiculturalism with the issue of nonwhite immigration. "The combined forces of open immigration and multiculturalism constitute a mortal threat to American civilization," he said. "The U.S. is receiving a never-ending mass immigration of non-Western peoples, leading inexorably to white-minority status in the coming decades [while] a race-based cultural diversity is attacking, with almost effortless success, the legitimacy of our Western culture."[28]

Defending the Canon: Allan Bloom and E. D. Hirsch

Among those who have spoken against multicultural curricula and practices, two individuals in particular have received tremendous publicity—the late Allan Bloom, a professor of philosophy at the University of Chicago best known for his work on Plato, and E. D. Hirsch, Jr., a professor of English at the University of Virginia. Both authors became well known for best-selling books: Bloom's *The Closing of the American Mind* and Hirsch's *Cultural Literacy: What Every American Needs to Know*.[29] Harking back to the conception of education propounded by the 1893 *Committee of Ten Report* that Dewey had rejected, both Bloom and Hirsch lament what they see as the decline of traditional standards in education: traditional assumptions about what is worthwhile and necessary to know, traditional cultural referents, and traditional Western values they claim are (or should be) sacred to all. Though these critics differ in significant ways, they share an overriding concern that a cultural consensus on values is vital to maintain the social cohesion needed to hold together the tremendously diverse American polity.

Bloom charges that the present-day purpose of American education is "not to make [students] scholars but to provide them with a moral virtue—openness."[30] Grouping together diverse cultural and political developments in contemporary American society—heightened attention to issues of class, race, and gender; the rejection of ethnocentrism coupled with a growing commitment to learning about other cultures; a critical reappraisal of U.S. history—Bloom charges "openness" with dislodging our moral moorings. Instead of providing an ethical framework that guides the emotional and intellectual development of today's students, openness fosters radical "moral relativism," "preventing us from talking with any conviction about good and evil" and leaving us with "no shared goals or vision of the public good."[31] This "shared vision"—now lost—posits the universal centrality of Western values and norms:

> Cultural relativism succeeds in destroying the West's universal or intellectually imperialistic claims, leaving it to be just another culture. So there is equality in the republic of cultures. Unfortunately the West is defined by its need for justification of its ways or values, by its need for discovery of nature, by its need for philosophy and science. This is its cultural imperative. Deprived of that, it will collapse. The United States is one of the highest and most extreme achievements of the rational quest for the good life according to nature. . . . It is important to emphasize that the lesson the students are drawing from their studies is simply untrue.[32]

Bloom also argues against the critical reappraisal of American history proffered by educators stretching from the Progressive era to the 1960s. He charges that Dewey saw "the past as radically imperfect and regarded our history as irrelevant," and accuses the "radicals in the civil rights movement" of "promoting a popular conviction that the Founding was, and the American principles are, racist." "Thus," he concludes, "openness has driven out the local deities, leaving only the speechless, meaningless country."[33]

Like Bloom, Hirsch also believes that Western cultural values should be privileged in the American school curriculum—not because they are inherently better, however, but because they offer shared cultural referents that he considers necessary for communicating across racial, class, and ethnic lines. Locating himself squarely within historical educational debates, Hirsch contends that "Dewey was deeply mistaken to disdain accumulating information in the form of symbols. Only by accumulating shared symbols, and the shared information that the symbols represent, can we learn to communicate effectively with one another in our national community."[34]

Like the 1893 *Committee of Ten* report with which he identifies, Hirsch calls for reinstating a traditional canon of "names, phrases, dates, and concepts" that every "culturally literate" American should know.[35] Rather than conceiving of this return to tradition as a challenge to democratic values, Hirsch claims it is the very "antidote to the deprivation" of "less privileged children."[36] Thus, though he speaks in terms that are quite different from Dewey's, Hirsch ironically appeals to the same democratic vision to argue his case: "The inherent conservatism of literacy leads to a subtle but unavoidable paradox: the goals of political liberalism require educational conservatism. We make social and economic progress *only* by teaching myths and facts that are predominantly traditional. . . . The civic importance of cultural literacy lies in the fact that true enfranchisement depends upon knowledge, knowledge upon literacy, and literacy upon cultural literacy."[37]

Hirsch shares with Bloom a critique of recent educational trends that "stress the virtue of multicultural education." But unlike his colleague, Hirsch laments time spent on teaching the values, canons, and concepts of other cultures not because this engenders cultural relativism, but because it detracts from "the primary and fundamental . . . acculturative responsibility of the schools."[38] He objects, also, to the critical methodology often employed by multicultural and related curricula, arguing not that the emphasis on cultural tolerance is dangerous, but that it is a distraction from teaching the more fundamental, "socially enabling" kinds of "knowledge": "The well-meaning . . . 'critical thinking' movement . . . aims to take children beyond the minimal basic skills mandated by state guidelines and to encourage the teaching of 'higher order' skills. Admirable as these goals are, the denigration of 'mere facts' by the movement's proponents is a dangerous

repetition of the mistakes of 1918. . . . Any movement that dep-
recates facts as antiquated or irrelevant injures the cause of higher
national literacy."[39]

Hirsch conceives of his educational mandate as apolitical. He
notes that American myths like George Washington chopping
down the cherry tree are produced and kept alive by cultural
mythology, believing that they "owe their longevity to human uni-
versality rather than conscious political design."[40] He urges schools
to teach these "shared symbols" to American youth but is wary
about teaching how to critically appraise them. His perspective thus
says as much about *how* we should come to know something as
about *what* we should come to know. Regarding the uncritical accu-
mulation of knowledge as a wholly unideological endeavor, he
notes: "A chief goal of cultural politics is to change the content and
values of culture. But the principal aim of schooling is to promote
literacy as an enabling competence. Although our public schools
have a duty to teach widely accepted cultural values, they have a
duty *not* to take political stands on matters that are subjects of con-
tinuing debate."[41]

Hirsch's conceptualization of education is, of course, not really
apolitical, as he claims. Nearly a century's worth of debates over values curricula attest to education's role as an arena for conflicting
views about the nature of American society and the means necessary for preserving democracy. Hirsch himself calls for a return to
the traditional Western canon of knowledge, claiming that this
canon is "classless, . . . [an] instrument of communication among
diverse cultures rather than a cultural or class instrument in its own
right." He also believes his cultural literacy endeavor to be "the
most democratic in the land."[42] But Hirsch's famous "list" of 5,000
terms implicitly buttresses a traditional and uncritical approach to
knowledge. Arguing for his list's political neutrality, he fails to recognize that the canons he celebrates are inherently political con-
structs that serve certain class, race, and gender interests over
others; that the "national" vocabulary is not neutral, but rather
reflects the discursive imprint of a dominant social order; and that

its continued reproduction has both political and social effects. Thus, though both he and Bloom condemn the politicization of the curriculum and conceive of their own project in apolitical terms, both implicitly further a conservative political agenda.

Right-wing critics of values-oriented curricula generally share the educational perspectives offered by the more moderate Bloom and Hirsch but unhesitatingly define their own project in political terms. As we will see in the next chapter, Eagle Forum president Phyllis Schlafly incorporates much of Bloom and Hirsch's critique in her argument against the Facing History and Ourselves program. To better understand Schlafly's critique and Facing History's response, it may be helpful to look first at how the FHAO organization defines its own educational mission and to situate that mission in relation to the curricular theorists and approaches already discussed. For like all educational initiatives, Facing History is in part the product of the curricular innovations that have come before it; in developing its own approach to fostering ethical thinking in American youth, it both builds on and diverges from earlier attempts to promote critical moral thinking in the schools.

Complicating Students' Thinking: The Antecedents and Mission of Facing History and Ourselves

Whether curriculum designers, teachers, or administrators, proponents of the Facing History and Ourselves approach believe that education must stimulate students to think critically and to act responsibly. This does not mean, however, that they see cognitive development and critical thinking as mutually exclusive. Rather, cognitive development is seen to emerge through a process of critical inquiry rooted in a rigorous study of a specific historical period. FHAO is primarily intended for adolescent students. Supporters claim that adolescents are not only capable of wrestling with the complex moral issues raised by the course, but that they are also in need of curricula that give voice to their own internal moral struggles. The encouragement of critical reflection on moral values, in turn, is seen as central to the democratic enterprise. FHAO contends that it promotes citizenship by helping students draw connections between historical acts of genocide and contemporary actions of individuals and governments.

Curriculum developers trace their educational philosophy to an eclectic group of psychologists, philosophers, and educators, among them John Dewey, Jean Piaget, Lawrence Kohlberg, and Hannah Arendt. Inspired by Arendt's question, "Could the activity of thinking, as such . . . be among the conditions that make men [sic] abstain from evil-doing or even actually condition them against it?," the program's architects urge civic responsibility not by imposing a set of dogmas on their students, but by challenging students to think independently and reflexively.[43] Influenced, too, by Kohlberg's understanding of what constitutes moral growth, Facing History's classroom methodology "encourage[s] students to understand more than one perspective in a dilemma, to place themselves in the position of another person, and to be willing to express ideas in class without fear of ridicule. Lessons are designed to encourage students to think about history and its relationship to their lives and to consider the consequences of decisions and actions as they explore the roles and responses of individuals and groups confronting difficult moral issues and dilemmas. They are challenged to complicate their thinking by not accepting simple solutions to complex questions of human behavior and history."[44]

Program designers contend that adolescents are uniquely suited to engage in this kind of inquiry. In developing the FHAO curriculum, they have built on Piaget's finding that with adolescence comes a significant shift in cognitive development—specifically, the ability to reason abstractly for the first time. Course designers hope to stimulate complex cognitive growth as well as moral thinking and action—in Facing History's own words, to help students "think about thinking." The program also seeks to attend to the emotional needs of adolescents. As Executive Director Margot Stern Strom argued to members of Congress when defending her program, adolescents "struggle with issues of trust, loyalty, and

responsibility as individuals within groups."[45] These personal struggles are given concrete shape in the Holocaust case study, where
students explore how average German citizens contended with
related psychological issues. Using both peer discussions and personal journals, the course uses a seemingly removed, historical
study to provide intellectual tools and a vehicle for dealing with
adolescent confusion, rage, and despair. As stated by the Facing
History *Resource Book*: "Adolescence is a time of major developmental transitions. The sort of moral reasoning which ought to be
a basic component of adolescent education and which is integral
to Facing History, nourishes critical, intellectual, social, and ethical development."[46]

Facing History also insists that its curriculum is neither relativistic nor indoctrinating. The program encourages students to
make ethical judgments based on the knowledge that human
behavior is contingent and context-bound, that lofty ideals must
ultimately be rooted in the actions of real individuals, and that real
individuals must continually reflect on their own actions vis-à-vis
their ideals. In this respect, the program invites the Right's charge of
"secular humanism," though it self-consciously rejects the label of
relativism. Unlike values clarification's radical personalism but sharing that approach's insistence on clear thinking, Facing History
seeks always to demonstrate that one's actions have an impact on
one's community. Unlike the hypothetical dilemmas that are the
mark of Kohlberg's method but sharing Kohlberg's focus on situations of moral conflict, the program utilizes actual events in history
to help students reflect on the dilemmas individuals have had to
face. "We do not teach relativism," Strom argues in response to the
Right's attack against Facing History's moral mission, but instead
"the application of basic values—good is good and evil is evil—in
the complex and challenging situations which characterize life in
modern civilization."[47]

The program's clear and consistent rejection of all forms of
racism, prejudice, and discrimination is illustrative in this regard,
as is a *Resource Book* segment not addressed in my earlier class-

room portraits but read and discussed by students during the semester. This segment asks students to analyze the objectives of Nazi education in light of "their own education in America today." "What do educators want students to learn?" the text asks. "What do parents want their children to learn? What do you think American students should learn? What is the role of education in American society?"[48] Questions like these are typical of Facing History pedagogy: in line with Dewey, they teach students about the past by making it relevant to their present; echoing values clarification, they help students identify their own values and beliefs in light of parental and societal expectations; differing from Kohlberg, they root critical reflection in lived historical realities, not hypothesized moral dilemmas. Students are directed to examine the actions of a society through first examining issues of individual responsibility, and as a result, both thinking and feeling are brought into the classroom.

From Facing History's perspective, then, the purpose of education is not simply to nurture cognitive development, but also to instill good moral character in students. A message sent annually by a principal to the teachers of his school makes this point adroitly. Reprinted in the FHAO *Resource Book,* the principal (who is also a Holocaust survivor) writes,

> Dear Teacher,
> I am a survivor of a concentration camp. My eyes saw what no man should witness. Gas chambers built by learned engineers. Children poisoned by educated physicians. . . . Women and babies shot and burned by high school and college graduates. So, I am suspicious of education. My request is: Help your students become human. Your efforts must never produce learned monsters, skilled psychopaths, educated Eichmanns. Reading, writing, arithmetic are important only if they serve to make our children more humane.[49]

Facing History's supporters equate being "more humane" with holding certain "prosocial" values. Responsive to the current multicultural turn, the values FHAO promotes include an increased awareness and tolerance of cultures different from one's own; knowledge of power inequities among diverse human groups and a commitment to easing those inequities; and a disinclination toward violence, coupled with a disposition toward critical reflection.

Though some New Right and conservative critics have charged that these values jeopardize social cohesion and denigrate American democracy, Facing History roots them squarely within the democratic tradition of protest and critique. The program seeks to foster not only an understanding of diverse ways of life, but also an understanding that lofty "American" goals will only be actualized by the actions of individuals. Executive Director Strom argues that this approach is "based upon an ancient and rigorous approach to citizenship education." Speaking before members of Congress when the program was under attack, she said: "We suggest a method of inquiry which stimulates students to examine and re-examine their assumptions and the assumptions of others so they can make the type of informed choices necessary for preserving our democratic institutions."[50]

We have already seen this approach manifested in the classroom. For example, twelve-year-old Amiri reflects it when he says of his classroom and school, "People are always arguing with the teacher, not only about things that she's teaching, but other things, you know. They don't just get everything just from the books. They don't believe, we don't believe, everything we hear."

In keeping with the ground rules laid down by the classroom teacher early on in the course (Marysa: "There will be no putdowns of other people. Even if people say things you disagree with, you need to give them your respect"), Amiri and his classmates are instructed that critical debate is essential to democracy. "The First Amendment protects everybody's rights," Marysa reminds Abby in the discussion catalyzed by the Klan youth film, and later, "You can't just say that the only ones who can speak are those who agree with your position!" To Josh, Marysa also explains: "The way to respond to problems is not to refuse to speak to someone, but to talk together to try to figure it out and to help people to change their beliefs."

Affirming these values and, like Hirsch and Bloom, casting them in apolitical terms, Strom eventually argued to members of Congress: "We regard our program as pro-democratic and pro-American. . . . We are not politicians, nor philosophers, we are educators who believe that schools can serve a valuable role in helping eradicate the vestiges of prejudice and bigotry from American society, and that the history of the Holocaust . . . offers a powerful lesson in this regard."[51]

But who defines what it means to be "pro-democratic" and "pro-American"? Even more fundamentally, who defines what either "American" or "democracy" actually means? As the battle over the Rugg textbooks in the 1930s and 1940s so clearly demonstrates, individuals have vastly different visions of both of these terms. Rugg regarded his texts as "pro-democratic" and "pro-American" because he sought to engage students in critical thinking about key American problems; Rugg's opponents considered his texts subversive and anti-American for just that reason.

Decades later, the battle over Facing History and Ourselves involved similarly conflicting visions and definitions. Like the Rugg controversy and like the debates spurred by the various curricular initiatives already discussed, the struggle over Facing History attests to public education's perceived role in shaping both individual and national character. It shows, once again, how debates about what schools should be doing and how they should be doing it are inextricably bound up with broader debates over who we are as a nation and the direction in which we should be going. Like the earlier curricular battles, the Facing History case also reveals the lack of a public consensus over the meaning of these important issues. And it shows that the outcome of battles over American schooling is often the result of complex and highly political interactions among members of the press, politicians, organized citizens' groups, and individual citizens.

However, as we will see in the next chapter, the Facing History

story also shows that these complex and critical debates are often fought out in veiled terms. The arenas in which they are debated and the terms in which they are discussed do not always allow for clear and direct discourse; as a result, the outcomes achieved are at times unclear and contradictory.

Chapter Six

The Fight Against Critical Moral Education

"When my daughter was 12 years old, she was given a questionnaire by her 7th grade health teacher without my knowledge or consent," began Gail T. Bjork, a concerned mother who spoke out at day-long hearings on "ethical responsibility in education" convened by the U.S. Department of Education in March 1984. "She was asked many personal questions, including being required to give her views about life after death. . . . You cannot convince me of any positive benefits of this approach to controversial subjects thrust upon unsuspecting minors. The manner in which these questions were presented to my child was not only an invasion of privacy, but violated the deepest moral and ethical teachings of our home."

Bjork was one of hundreds of parents who lined up behind microphones in seven U.S. cities (Concord, New Hampshire; Kansas City, Missouri; Orlando, Florida; Phoenix, Arizona; Pittsburgh, Pennsylvania; Seattle, Washington; Washington, D.C.) to protest what they saw as the wrong direction in which American education was headed. Inspired and in part organized by Phyllis Schlafly's Eagle Forum and other New Right organizations, the hearings were designed to gather evidence to substantiate the need for regulations implementing the 1978 Protection of Pupil Rights statute, which prohibited schools from using curricula deemed "psychologically invasive" without prior parental approval. The hearings were held toward the end of Ronald Reagan's first term in office and reflected the spirit of the "Reagan revolution" afoot in a variety of social, political, and cultural arenas, including education. They also provided a forum for voicing New Right charges against social and cultural trends in American society at large, and in its public schools in particular.

Marcy Meenan, a distressed mother from Pittsburgh, complained to Department of Education officials at the hearings that "open-ended sentences pry into the personal area of the child's beliefs. Questions are asked with no correct answer provided, implanting dishonest values. . . . [And] plays presented to students with actors dancing on the United States Flag are not uncommon and were a big problem here. . . . Kids are definitely being programmed to accept a new global perspective." "Is it any wonder that our children in this nation cannot read, write, or count, when so much time is spent in our nation's classrooms on such activities?" Snookie Dellinger asked. "This type of education has produced young people whose way of life and actions are destructive to our society and to the human spirit," argued Frances Reilly, another concerned mother.[1]

To ensure the widest possible audience for these heated charges, Phyllis Schlafly published *Child Abuse in the Classroom*, a compilation of parents' testimony that was distributed by the Eagle Forum.[2] The book argued that the myriad complaints registered by parents around the nation proved that "federally-funded curricula have invaded the privacy of the child and his family and have deliberately attempted to change the religious, moral, and political attitudes of public schoolchildren. No wonder so many children are emotionally confused, alienated from their parents, detached from moral standards, and are functional illiterates."[3]

The book's conclusions were shared by right-wing forces during Reagan's tenure. Alleging that under the Carter administration, liberals had come to dominate the Department of Education, right-wing groups moved during the Reagan years from the fringes to the center of educational policy-making. Many opposed "big government" and wanted educational policy set at the local rather than the federal level. Many also feared that a growing Soviet threat endangered America's security, and so argued that priority in federal spending should be given to the military rather than social programs. Some even argued that the Department of Education should be dismantled or at the least drastically reduced in size and scope.

Reagan came into office partially beholden to the New Right, since his election was in part due to the tireless efforts of New Right organizers. Paul Weyrich, Howard Phillips, and Richard Viguerie helped raised more than $20 million for the 1980 Republican campaign, and grassroots groups like the Eagle Forum, the Moral Majority, and Gun Owners of America mobilized their constituencies to support Reagan and to defeat liberal candidates. Though some New Right leaders would criticize the new president for favoring traditional establishment conservatives over those further to the right, Reagan in fact appointed several of the movement's leaders to government posts, among them James Watt as Secretary of the Interior and C. Everett Koop, a staunch opponent of abortion rights, as Surgeon-General.[4]

Reagan campaigned on a pledge to abolish the Department of Education once in office. Though his promise went unfulfilled due to the political resistance he encountered, the president decimated funds for educational programs and ensured that his own political priorities were met, in large part through placing numerous political appointees in office. As his Secretary of Education, Reagan appointed William Bennett, a man so sure of his own conservative credentials that he willingly submitted to an "ideological screening" by New Right leaders during his nomination proceedings. As *Nation* columnist Christopher Hitchens noted, after Bennett met with representatives from the Eagle Forum, the Moral Majority, the Conservative Caucus, and the Committee for the Survival of a Free Congress, New Right leaders confidently reported that "[Reagan's] appointment of William Bennett as [Secretary] . . . is a clear indication that the President understands who his friends are."[5]

Once in office, Bennett did not let the New Right down. He appeared on Pat Robertson's "700 Club" television show and urged parents to protest their schools' curriculum. He spoke to the Carolina Policy Council, a right-wing organization hostile to the very concept of public education. And he oversaw the appointment of numerous right-wing ideologues to department posts. Among them were William Kristol as chief of staff; Donald Senese as Assistant Secretary of Education; Rosemary Thomson, a former leader of the Eagle Forum, as special assistant; Eileen Gardner of the Heritage Foundation as head of the Office of Educational Philosophy and Practice; New Right spokesman Gary Bauer as Deputy Under Secretary; and Robert Billings, a former executive director of the Moral Majority, as the overseer of the department's ten regional offices.

These appointees made no secret of their views. For example, Robert Billings gave wide circulation to a memo in which, Christopher Hitchens reported, he "complain[ed] that 'godlessness' was taking over America, once a 'Christian nation,'" and openly "advocat[ed] fundamentalist private schools."[6] And Gary Bauer, who was reportedly enamored of "The Cosby Show" because it showed traditional family relations, principally "children re-spect[ing] their father," argued that the "values taught on the Cosby show would do more to help low-income and minority children than a bevy of new Federal programs."[7]

Reagan's political appointees within the Department of Education created a chilly climate for educational programs they deemed politically subversive, anti-American, and dangerous. And the Facing History and Ourselves curriculum was chief among the programs they attacked, motivated by Schlafly's targeting of the pro-gram in the 1984 hearings on ethical responsibility in education.

The heated opposition to Facing History merits discussion since it is representative of the Right's long-standing criticism of efforts to promote critical moral reasoning in the schools. There were spe-cific aspects of the Facing History program that particularly aroused Phyllis Schlafly's ire, but her criticisms of the program were part of a broader campaign that also targeted many other curricula. Schlafly's objections to Facing History were virtually identical to many of the charges leveled against programs dating back to the 1940s, though they were of course updated to fit changed circum-stances. To be properly understood, then, Schlafly's opposition to

Facing History must be seen as simply one instance of a much broader critique. Nor should her campaign be seen as a solitary endeavor, but rather one in which many segments of the Right joined and that had roots in much older battles around education.

Analysis of this particular curriculum battle shows how the Right has systematically organized—in many instances successfully—to rid schools of these kinds of programs. It also brings into sharper relief the constellation of "traditional values" the New Right seeks to impose in the schools and elsewhere. And it illuminates issues that are at times of concern to a politically broader group of parents.

Equally important, the battle over Facing History illustrates how decisions regarding key educational issues are so often inextricably bound up with conflicting visions of American society and its future. Tellingly, however, the terms in which the Facing History debate was cast often elided these fundamental issues, in keeping with a distinctive tendency in American culture and politics to posit a consensual democratic ideal that transcends divisive ideologies and political and cultural differences. One cannot help but wonder how much the outcome of the battle over Facing History was affected by the debate surrounding the curriculum—a debate at times largely incidental to the key issues at stake—in which members of the press, Congress, and concerned citizens groups all ultimately became engaged. An analysis of how this particular curriculum battle unfolded thus sheds as much light on the cultural dynamics that underlie educational decision making in American society as it does on the politics of the decisions themselves.

"Child Abuse in the Classroom": Phyllis Schlafly's Educational Vision

What, then, was Schlafly's own vision of an educational program suitable for American youth? What, specifically, were her arguments against Facing History and Ourselves? And how did she go about organizing against the program?

First and foremost, Schlafly and her colleagues conceived of childhood and adolescence as a time of innocence, not struggle. In contrast to proponents of Facing History and Ourselves and related moral education curricula, she argued for protecting students from controversial, conflictual, and potentially confusing subject matter. She warned that engagement with such material could "depress the child," "lead[ing] him to a negative view of himself, his family, his country, or his future." Hoping to shield children from real-world problems, she found fault with programs that asked students to critically appraise complex or controversial subject matter such as contemporary violence, racism, or antisemitism. "Does [a program] produce fear, guilt, and despair?" she asked by way of supplying parents with guidelines for determining a curriculum's potential for damage. "Is it preoccupied with death and tragedy? Does it encourage the child to dwell on unhappy or tragic events . . . ? Does it force the child to confront adult problems which are too complex and unsuitable for his tender years . . . ?"[8]

To demonstrate how heavy and "unsuitable" a burden Facing History placed on its students, Schlafly cited what she saw as incriminating comments made by students themselves in journals they kept as part of the course and later published in an analysis of the curriculum. As we will see in more detail later, the students' comments that she used to support her argument were partial fragments of journal entries chosen selectively and taken out of context. "I feel as though something I have had all my life has been taken away from me, something that can never be totally restored," one student was reputed to have written. "We all, in our struggling humanity, have to clutch to our eyeballs to keep out the cold light of despair."[9] Such comments painted a highly distorted picture of the course and portrayed students as being distraught and overwhelmed by program material. Having (at best) misunderstood or (at worst) deliberately manipulated students' comments, Schlafly was able to argue that Facing History's disturbing subject matter caused real psychological harm. In this respect, she argued, the program violated the 1978 statute protecting pupils' rights.

In Schlafly's opinion, other dimensions of the course also violated the statute's spirit. The curriculum's use of a personal journal,
for example, was regarded as a serious invasion of the child's (and
by extension, the parents') privacy rather than an invaluable safe
space for private reflection, as Facing History believed. "Writing a
journal encourages the child to share his innermost thoughts and
feelings with some adult in the school administration . . . rather
than with his parents," Schlafly argued in the February 1984 issue
of the *Phyllis Schlafly Report*. "This kind of journal writing is a griev-
ous invasion of the child's privacy. It encourages the child to report
events and attitudes within the home that are clearly none of the
school's business."[10]

In her testimony at the ethical responsibility hearings, Schlafly
charged FHAO and other forms of "therapy education" with using
an intentionally elusive discourse "to prevent parents from understanding either the[ir] purposes or the[ir] methodology." In-
comprehensible and alienating terms like "values-clarification,"
"moral reasoning," and "decision-making" are intended to wrest
control of children's education away from parents, where it right-
fully belongs. Reclaiming parental control of the educational
agenda is "*the* civil rights issue of the 1980s," she argued in *Child
Abuse in the Classroom*.[11]

Exactly why was it imperative that parents regain their place at
the helm? Because the invasion of a student's—and parents'—
privacy is not neutral, but allegedly a deliberate attempt to drive a
wedge between students and their God-fearing parents, supplant-
ing the parents' values with the "secular humanism" now rampant
in the schools. On the basis of testimony parents offered at the hearings, Schlafly argued that "children are taught in a thousand ways
that parents are old-fashioned and often (or even usually) wrong.
They are taught that situation ethics is the norm in today's pluralistic society, and that a child who maintains religious values is somehow out of step with today's secular society."[12]

Many in the New Right were sharply critical of what they
deemed as morally relativist thinking and held it responsible for

causing widespread depression among American youth. Relativist thinking, Schlafly argued in *Child Abuse in the Classroom*, accounts for "why children are so emotionally and morally confused" and why we are "experiencing high rates of teenage suicide, loneliness, premarital sex, and pregnancies."[13] In the Department of Education hearings, Schlafly again selectively quoted Facing History's own students as evidence of this disturbing development: "I have learned that there is seldom a right or wrong but rather a right and a left," one student purportedly declared. Another wrote, "I'm conscious of having changed in the strength of my convictions on many of the ethical dilemmas we've confronted. But in other ways I'm less sure of myself and more introspective. Where do I draw the line between right and wrong?"[14]

To those on the Right, the line between right and wrong could never be blurred, but was instead a clearly delineated divide between the forces of good and evil as determined by absolute, Judeo-Christian principles. The "traditional values" movement of the New Right has been marked by an unquestioned and uncritical belief in God and country and sees itself as opposed to secular humanism, liberalism, communism, globalism, multiculturalism, and a host of other "isms" believed to undermine faith in individualism, patriotism, and laissez-faire capitalism. Chip Berlet and Margaret Quigley have noted in their lucid discussion of the New Right movement that "traditional values start from a recognition of the absolute, unchanging, hierarchical authority of God . . . and move from there to a belief in hierarchical arrangements in the home and state. As Pat Robertson said at the [1988] Republican convention, 'Since I have come to Houston, I have been asked repeatedly to define traditional values. I say very simply, to me and to most Republicans, traditional values start with faith in Almighty God.' "[15]

This unshaken belief in their interpretation of Judeo-Christian values is integrally connected to a belief in the superiority of Western civilization, a premise the Right regards as critical to impart to American youth. According to the Institute for Cultural Conservatism, a conservative think tank that works closely with the Heritage Foundation, cultural conservatism is "the belief that there is a necessary, unbreakable, and causal relationship between traditional Western, Judeo-Christian values, definitions of right and wrong, ways of thinking and ways of living, the parameters of Western culture—and the secular success of Western societies: their prosperity, their liberties, and the opportunities they offer their citizens to lead fulfilling, rewarding lives. If the former are abandoned, the latter will be lost."[16]

In this context, only parents—and more particularly, only good Christian parents—can be trusted to teach the right values to their children. Teaching the "right" values means teaching not only that moral standards (as the New Right defines them) are absolute, but also that only American and Judeo-Christian standards are moral. "What's wrong with global education?" Schlafly asked. "[It] indoctrinat[es] the error of equivalence, that is, the falsehood that other nations, governments, legal systems, cultures, and political and economic systems are essentially equivalent to ours and entitled to equal respect. This hypothesis is false, both historically and morally."[17]

Schlafly saw values as absolute, not relative or determined by human standards or by time and place. She consequently regarded courses that promote "a constant questioning of values, standards, and authority"[18] as "radical ethical relativism."[19] Consistent with the ideology of the New Right, she saw Western culture as sacrosanct, the American free enterprise system as inherently superior to socialism,[20] and the nuclear bomb as "a marvelous gift from a wise and wonderful God to America."[21] Courses like Facing History that attempt to stimulate ethical inquiry "promot[e] pacifism" and "present moral right and wrong as being variables, which is dead wrong."[22] In keeping with the view that children are not able to handle complex problems, that parental authority should remain supreme, and that certain values are absolute, New Right critics regarded the endeavor to problematize moral thinking as itself immoral.

Finally, as if this "immorality" were not bad enough, Schlafly complained that class time spent on "feelings and attitudes" detracted from time required for "teaching knowledge, facts, and traditional basic skills."[23] Like the attack against the Progressive educational movement in the 1940s, 1950s, and 1960s, today's New Right leaders decry schools' focus on contemporary social issues and advocate a return to curricular basics. Schlafly herself regarded cognitive development and critical thinking to be at cross-purposes. To add historical weight to her argument, she contended that "the originators of 'therapy' education began peddling their notions in the 1930s about the same time that the teaching of reading started its steep decline."[24] "Let's get back to 'basic skills' and 'what works,'" she wrote in 1987 to then–Department of Education chief of staff William Kristol.

As we saw briefly in the last chapter, Schlafly was in good company in holding the "liberalization" of the curriculum responsible for the "failure" of American schools. In criticizing "therapy education," she built upon then–Education Secretary William Bennett's call to "return to the basics" and E. D. Hirsch, Jr.'s call to promote "cultural literacy." An issue of the *Education Reporter* (another publication of the Eagle Forum) located opposition to FHAO squarely within contemporary debates about declining educational standards, moral openness, and multiculturalism—issues of concern to parents who might not otherwise align themselves with the Right's agenda. The *Reporter* named Hirsch's *Dictionary of Cultural Literacy* its choice for "book of the month" and reprinted a *Washington Times* story that attacked college-level initiatives similar to those of the Facing History program: "The rush by colleges to . . . poke and prod individual psyches on such touchy topics as racial prejudices and homophobia is sweeping the campuses in tandem with a growing institutional inclination to make the study of non-Western culture an academic requirement."[25]

The same article went on to quote William Kristol as saying, "Colleges would be better off paying attention to old-fashioned character building and simply telling students that certain behavior is wrong."[26] In agreement with Kristol, New Right ideologues urged a new relationship between government and local school agencies, one that would radically reduce the federal role in educational decision making. Summing up the import of the 1984 Department of Education hearings, Schlafly asserted: "These witnesses prove that Federal funding is NOT the solution for education problems but the CAUSE of those problems. Psychological abuse of children in the classroom is a national disease carried to every state by the Typhoid Marys of Federal funding. Any politician who recommends more Federal spending on schools is spreading the disease, not curing it. The American people must understand this in 1984."[27]

"The Civil Rights Issue of the 1980s": The New Right and Public Education

In the 1980s, as part of their attempt to curtail federal spending and to turn educational policy around, New Right forces sought to take over or dismantle many divisions of the Department of Education. The Education Department's "National Diffusion Network" (NDN) was particularly vulnerable because it was created and funded by departmental decision rather than by congressional mandate. Established in 1974 by the Nixon administration, the NDN was designed to help local school systems nationwide become aware of effective educational programs used elsewhere in the country. To this day, the Network helps educators evaluate, develop, and disseminate information about "educational programs that work." Programs seeking wider distribution may apply to the NDN to be reviewed by a panel of educational experts. If deemed educationally effective by these reviewers, a program is "validated" for a renewable six-year period; information about the program is then disseminated to school systems across the country. The Network is designed to help those who develop programs as well as those who may potentially use them.

Throughout the 1980s, New Right critics opposed both the process through which NDN program evaluations were made and the content of the courses approved by NDN reviewers. Seeking to protect what they regarded as the rights of parents and local school authorities, New Right forces argued against entrusting the evaluation of educational excellence to a select group of individuals. Concerned, too, that liberals controlled the Education Department and dominated the NDN review process, they charged the division with validating programs bent on changing the moral attitudes of American youth. "Do you understand the significance of this National Diffusion Network?," ultraright critic Barbara Morris asked in her self-published 1979 pamphlet, *Change Agents in the Schools: Destroy Your Children, Betray Your Country.* "It means," according to Morris, "that an elite corps of 22 change agents in Washington decide what federal programs will be promoted and disseminated throughout schools—government and nongovernment alike. The 22 change agents, who are chosen '. . . for their ability to analyze the effectiveness of educational programs,' have the power to select and fund, without benefit of public participation or parental involvement, without any accountability—what programs will go into schools. . . . The current . . . selected programs represent just the beginning of a totally nationalized school system."[28]

Morris pointed accusingly to a curriculum titled "Meeting Modern Problems" as an example of the subversive "change agent" forces at work. This program is "indeed psychotherapy and a whole lot more," she charged. "It uses values clarification, produces parent-child alienation and promotes the worst kind of political indoctrination." Foreshadowing Schlafly's testimony at the Department of Education hearings a few years later, Morris proclaimed: "Now is the time for parents to demand access to classrooms and to investigate programs and activities used in classrooms to change children."[29]

Like other arms of the government, the NDN was not immune to the influence of Reagan's political appointees. Overseen by Donald Senese, Reagan's new Assistant Secretary of Education, NDN process and decision-making changed substantially during the Reagan years. For example, Senese cut the funding for thirteen "effective education" programs previously validated by the NDN almost immediately after he took office. The programs fought back, assisted by the National Dissemination Study Group, an educators' advocacy organization that monitors Department or Education activity. They filed a lawsuit against the department and worked tirelessly to alert members of Congress and the national press to what they perceived as department wrongdoing. But neither Congress nor the press initially showed much interest in the growing influence of right-wing forces, and the lawsuit ultimately proved unsuccessful. Educators inside and outside the Beltway, however, were gradually becoming aware that a sea change was taking place within the Department of Education.

"Unfair to Nazis"? The Attack on Facing History and Ourselves

Facing History and Ourselves stood in the cross-fire between liberal and New Right forces within the Department of Education throughout Reagan's second term as president, a target of New Right opposition and a victim of the Right's virtual takeover of the NDN and other agency bodies. When Schlafly called for an end to all NDN programs that "undermine parental authority, patriotism, religious faith, family cohesiveness, and sexual abstinence,"[30] Facing History and Ourselves may have been foremost in her mind.

When Facing History was validated in 1980, NDN reviewers labeled the program "exemplary" on the basis of its contribution to cognitive growth in seventh and eighth graders. Initially funded with Federal Elementary and Secondary Education Act (ESEA) Title IV monies, the program later sought funds directly from the NDN to be disseminated across the United States. The controversy surrounding Facing History took shape over these dissemination funds and began with FHAO Executive Director Margot Stern Strom's appointment to the NDN Advisory Council in 1985, just a short time after the Department of Education had held its hearings on "ethical responsibility in education."

Encouraged by liberals within the department who had been

organizing to save the NDN from the growing influence of the Right, FHAO applied for a three-year, $150,000 dissemination grant in 1986. But the strong approbation that marked FHAO's evaluation in 1980 was a far cry from reviewers' responses six years later. The reviewers were under the direction of Shirley Curry, a Reagan appointee who in January 1986 became the director of the NDN Recognition Division, the agency responsible for evaluating curricula and allocating dissemination funds. The evaluators found much to criticize in the Facing History proposal and categorically rejected its request for funds.

Since these reviewers were handpicked by Curry, it is not surprising that they gave the program such low marks. Curry was the former executive director of the Eagle Forum and remained an active member of the Eagle Forum's board of directors while in office at the department. She opposed Facing History and Ourselves for the same reasons Schlafly had publicly attacked it in the 1984 department hearings. Brought in by Reagan with Schlafly's blessing, Curry rightly saw her appointment as an opportunity to realize the New Right's political agenda in the educational domain. "I'm here because I was owed a political favor. My boys are at the bat, and I want to play," she announced at a February 1987 meeting of NDN groups. During Curry's tenure, all NDN meetings opened with a prayer and a salute to the flag.

Curry's impact was extensive. Her most far-reaching—though only temporarily successful—initiative involved changing the rules regarding the NDN's validation procedure. From its inception in 1974, the NDN had evaluated curricula solely on the basis of educational "effectiveness." In 1986, Curry introduced a second step in the review process: scrutiny of a course's "ethical content" by a new (and still provisional) "Program Significance Panel" (PSP) to determine whether it "would be generally acceptable to education service providers and parents."[31]

Judging from their comments about FHAO, members of the PSP were politically in tune with Curry and her New Right colleagues. As with other Department of Education reviewers in this period, they may have been selected more for their ideological leanings than for their educational expertise. Jean Narayanan, who took over as Recognition Director in 1993, recalls Curry looking through the résumés of potential reviewers for the Blue Ribbon Schools, another of the department's national recognition programs. "If she saw someone was affiliated with the League of Women Voters she'd say, 'Oh, no, that's a red flag! The American Association of University Women—that's a red flag!'" Reviewers brought in to assess programs falling under the guidelines of the Women's Educational Equity Act (WEEA) were also politically motivated. One reportedly told her hometown paper that she was "on her way to Washington to help curb a 'feminist agency' that Reagan wanted abolished." WEEA reviewers were also alarmingly ill-prepared to evaluate the programs on their roster. They "neither understood nor supported educational equity," noted Susan Faludi in *Backlash: The Undeclared War Against American Women*. "One reader, whose job was to review applications that would help enforce Title IX, asked the panel's moderator plaintively, 'What *is* Title IX?' Another woman, who was supposed to be reviewing applications to help disabled women, wanted to know if being a Native American qualified as a 'disability.'"[32]

Some of the reviewers on Curry's panel made equally disturbing comments about the Facing History program. Perhaps the most astonishing were those attributed to Christina Price, at that time a political scientist at Troy State University in Alabama and later a lecturer at Kennesaw College in Marietta, Georgia. Leaked to Strom by a sympathizer within the Department of Education, Price's evaluation noted: "The program gives no evidence of balance or objectivity. The Nazi point of view, however unpopular, is still a point of view and is not presented, nor is that of the Ku Klux Klan."

Price also voiced a host of other criticisms against the program that were in keeping with long-standing New Right concerns. She suggested, for example, that the course would be more beneficial if it focused on countries with which the United States was in conflict rather than on countries in Western Europe (like the Federal

Republic of Germany) with which the United States was now closely allied. "The selection of only two problem areas, Germany and Armenia, leaves out many of which [sic] are more recent," she argued. "I'm thinking of the U.S.S.R., Afghanistan, Cambodia, and Ethiopia, among others." She also seems to have regarded the Holocaust as an exclusively "Jewish" problem, with no broader relevance for the majority of Americans. Facing History "may be appropriate for a limited religious audience," she said, "but not for wider distribution." Finally, Price saw the course's emphasis on critical thinking as an antiparent initiative bent on forcibly altering students' attitudes and beliefs. She remarked: "It is a paradoxical and strange aspect of this program [that] the methods used to change the thinking of students is the same that Hitler and Goebbels used to propagandize the German people. This reeducation method was perfected by Chairman Mao and now is being foisted on American children under the guise of 'understanding' history. It is demeaning to a free people."[33]

Though Strom considered Price's remarks outrageous and was alarmed by the right-wing bias of panel reviewers, she ultimately agreed to refrain from public protest at the request of a sympathizer within the Education Department. Arguing that the matter could best be handled internally and hoping to prevail in supporting certain programs regarded as liberal despite the New Right's efforts to the contrary, this well-positioned career official convinced FHAO to apply for dissemination funds a second time in the spring of 1987.

Round Two: Evaluating Program "Significance"

But Facing History's second funding request met with equally disastrous results. A second group of PSP reviewers, again handpicked by Curry, gave the program extremely low marks. Some charged that the program was "profoundly offensive to fundamentalists and evangelicals." Others complained that it made "selective use of leftist authorities," citing Kurt Vonnegut and *New York Times* columnist Flora Lewis as examples. Still others found it to be "anti-war, anti-hunting, and likely to induce a guilt trip."[34]

Phyllis Schlafly also weighed in to support panel members hostile to FHAO. To support Curry's efforts, she wrote directly to Education Department chief of staff William Kristol and urged his intervention in denying the program funds. To back up her allegations about the program's invasion of privacy, psychological manipulation, and induced behavior change, Schlafly relied on the same comments extracted from student journals that she had quoted three years earlier, at the department's public hearings on ethical responsibility. The program's "adverse, negative, and offensive psychological effects" are *revealed by those who taught, took, and evaluated the course,*" she wrote Kristol. "I emphasize that NONE of my information was taken from those who are critical of the curriculum. ALL my information is from supporters."[35]

Schlafly's disclaimer was true in only the strictest sense, for while she did quote certain words from entries in journals students kept while taking the course, she also left out a good many other words. By quoting students selectively and out of context, she successfully portrayed the course as having induced moral relativism, confusion, and despair—charges that lay at the heart of the New Right's opposition to values-oriented curricula since the early 1970s.

Schlafly's use of selective quotation becomes obvious if we put the passages she quoted (which appear here in italics) in her 1984 testimony and again in her 1987 letter back in the fuller text from which they were extracted.

Seeing how other people think and express their opinions *I have learned that there is seldom a right or wrong but rather a right or left.* This kind of learning is much more valuable than the factual kind of dates and definitions. The world is full of "subjective" people who know facts but live their lives according to their opinions.[36]

I feel as though something I have had all my life has been taken away from me, something that can never be totally restored. I almost feel that I need it back because I feel so awful without it. Perhaps it's a form of innocence, a removal of my protective blinders. *We all, in our struggling humanity, have to clutch to our eyeballs to keep out the cold light of despair.* Looking at things as they really are is a form of growing up.[37]

Where do I draw the line between right and wrong . . . , between acting responsibly and acting irresponsibly out of need? I'm still not sure but I know at least I am more aware of the need to consider such questions in my life.[38]

Thanks to the joint force of Schlafly's alarming letter and the PSP's hostile evaluation, Facing History and Ourselves was denied dissemination funds a second time in 1987.

Ironically enough, however, this second funding rejection proved to be the PSP's undoing. Bent on curtailing the Right's growing influence, liberals within the Department of Education leaked news of Facing History's 1986 and 1987 funding denials to the news media in the hope of building public opposition to the PSP. Their strategy proved effective. Curry's newly established PSP soon came under attack by those who feared it would lead to censorship as well as to the usurping of local control over the educational agenda.

An August 1987 article in *Education Week* reported that over 300 educators, public officials, and parents responded during a ten-day period in which members of the public were invited to comment on Curry's creation (still provisional) of the PSP and her introduction of ethical content as a criterion of evaluation. Two-thirds of these responses were critical. Many found it ironic that an administration that touted local control and a reduced role for government now favored placing decisions about the ethical value of curricula in federal, rather than local, hands. "It is hard to see how a panel could be expected to determine what over 16,000 school districts might find acceptable or unacceptable," the bipartisan leadership of the House Education and Labor Committee argued critically in a letter to Secretary of Education Bennett. The director of an NDN project in Mobile, Alabama, concurred: "I . . . am incensed that my government does not believe that I or my colleagues have the good sense to [distinguish] appropriate from inappropriate materials."[39]

Aware of the New Right's long-standing opposition to educational programs they considered detrimental to religious values, and cognizant that New Right leaders had voiced vociferous opposition to many NDN programs during the 1984 hearings on ethical responsibility, many educators feared Curry's PSP would in fact function as an ideological screen against courses the Right deemed "morally relativist," "secular humanist," or "antiparent." Max McConkey, director of the National Dissemination Study Group, underscored this fear when remarking that the 1987 decision to deny Facing History and Ourselves dissemination funds was "an example of what can happen if a program is blackballed for ideological reasons." "If a school doesn't want Facing History in its curriculum, it doesn't have to adopt it," McConkey said. "But if a local district finds that it meets their needs, [the program] should be available."[40] On the other hand, some factions seemed not only to have understood the PSP's underlying ideological purpose, but also to have embraced it. A group called the "Western Pennsylvania Parents to Protect Our Youth from Propaganda, Brainwashing, and Subversive Textbooks in Our Schools" commended the proposed inclusion of parents on the PSP.

But PSP advocates within the Department of Education flatly rejected the suggestion that their new panel was politically motivated. For example, Ronald Preston, a deputy assistant secretary in the Office of Educational Research and Improvement, argued, "We don't want a stilted [review] panel of right-wing ideologues. That would be dangerous for conservatives. What goes around comes around in this town." However, he also admitted that the department had "bungled" in bringing Christina Price onto the Facing History review panel and that in the future it would "try to have people who are a little more of the mainstream."[41] Preston claimed the significance review process had an unideological yet ethical purpose—to prevent ethically objectional programs from receiving "the federal imprimatur." "All we need is a program that promotes the

Ku Klux Klan to pass just because it was effective," he told a reporter for the *Washington Post*. "Then we'd have the whole city down around our ears."[42] Assistant Secretary of Education Chester E. Finn, Jr., went one step further in objecting to criticisms of the PSP's allegedly political nature. Rebutting a *Washington Post* editorial highly critical of the PSP, he argued that the panel had nothing whatsoever to do with evaluations of ethical content: "The Program Significance Panel judges that the content of an NDN program's product or practice is accurate and up to date, that it is appropriate to the grade level for which it is proposed, that it is educationally sound, and that it can be presented in a clear manner to teachers, students, and parents."[43]

The overwhelming majority of those aware of what Curry had done with regard to NDN procedure did not buy the department's defense, however. Lobbied extensively by NDN member groups under the direction of Max McConkey, 100 members of Congress wrote letters to the Department of Education opposing the creation of the PSP. Early in 1988, Congress voted 97 to 1 to disband the panel altogether.

Though media coverage of Facing History's funding denial brought attention to the PSP and indirectly contributed to its demise, there is a sense in which the media's role was less than helpful. When in the summer of 1987 *Education Week* broke news of Facing History's 1986 and 1987 funding denials, it emphasized reviewer Christina Price's inflammatory remarks. *Education Week* did its best to put Price's comments in the broader context of rightwing ideological influence within the department, but other media outlets did not always bother. Within a month of *Education Week*'s piece, the *New York Daily News* ran the Facing History story under a banner headline proclaiming "Unfair to Nazis." Soon scores of mainstream papers across the country were reporting on the Facing History debacle, emphasizing Price's outlandish comments and, to a greater or lesser extent, leveling charges of antisemitism against officials within the Department of Education. Though Curry, Price, and the other review panelists had found fault with Facing History on several grounds, and though their opposition and organizing tactics had reflected broader New Right concerns, most newspapers ignored these more complex political and intellectual issues and focused instead on the inflammatory issue of antisemitism.[44]

Concern over the ideological purpose of the PSP became entangled with, and ultimately eclipsed by, outrage over alleged antisemitism at the Department of Education. This in turn affected future action regarding the program. As Connecticut Senator Lowell Weicker argued convincingly before his colleagues during the PSP debate, "The antisemitic nature of [Price's] comments is deeply repugnant and has no place in a Federally sanctioned review."[45] When members of Congress voted overwhelmingly to disband the PSP early in 1988, they were simultaneously proclaiming their staunch opposition to antisemitism. That 1988 was an election year was probably no coincidence.

Round Three: Rejecting History, Claiming the Holocaust

Shamed by the critical media attention and pressured by Congress and ordinary citizens' groups to clean up its act, the Department of Education made a public apology to FHAO early in 1988 and urged the program to submit a third proposal for funding. That summer a third review was conducted by a new set of panel members who had not been picked by Curry. They ranked the program first in its funding category. One panelist remarked: "This is clearly one of the blue-ribbon curriculum projects in the country today. There is an admirable focus upon recorded history and a philosophical, literary, and artistic expression thereof. Unlike the 'values education' of Simon et al., which establishes an ethical no-man's land which is totally relativistic, students have moral discussions about real events and real people."[46]

Despite the glowing review, Curry remained committed to blocking funding for FHAO. She lobbied William Kristol directly, bypassing several of her Department of Education superiors who had flatly refused to deny Facing History funds for a third time. With Kristol's unwavering support, Curry determined not to fund any programs in the "History, Geography, and Civics" category in which Facing History had competed—an ironic decision since the new category had been proposed by Secretary Bennett himself. Five other funding categories were also denied funding, in what Max McConkey termed part of a cover-up.[47] Congressional and citizen opponents were furious but acknowledged that Curry's actions were in no way illegal, for NDN "announcements inviting awards carry the disclaimer that the department may not fund all the projects it has money for and may not fund projects in all categories."[48]

Politically speaking, this third rejection of funding could not have been more poorly timed. Just two months short of the 1988 presidential elections, the administration appeared increasingly vulnerable to the antisemitism charge. At about the same time that the media was reporting the third denial of funds to Facing History and Ourselves, news broke of links between antisemitic and/or formerly fascist groups and top advisers to George Bush's presidential campaign.[49] Reviewer Price's comments still lingered in the public memory, as did Reagan's decision to lay a commemorative wreath at a German cemetery in Bitburg where soldiers of World War II— among them members of the SS—lay buried. Though Reagan also ceremoniously set the cornerstone for the U.S. Holocaust Memorial in early October, this conciliatory and highly publicized act did little to assuage growing estrangement between Republican candidates and Jewish groups. Democratic members of the House called congressional hearings to look into the Facing History case a mere two weeks before the presidential elections, seeking to make the most of Republican vulnerability.

Charging the Reagan Education Department with antisemitism and stressing the importance of Holocaust education, members of Congress adopted the media's framing of the NDN controversy as an issue that primarily involved the Holocaust and that was of primary concern to Jewish individuals and groups. In so doing, they sidestepped the broader educational and moral purpose of the

Facing History course and minimized the New Right politics that underpinned the decision to deny it funds. In an October 1988 statement made before the House of Representatives and later submitted to the newly appointed Education Secretary Lauro Cavazos (who had replaced William Bennett when the latter was appointed "drug czar"), Representative Sidney R. Yates narrowly characterized Facing History as a program "dedicated to a study of the murder of six million Jews during the Holocaust by the Nazis."[50] One week later, New York Representative Ted Weiss opened congressional hearings on "the failure of the Department of Education to fund the Holocaust Project" by charging that "the Department's actions against Facing History suggests an institutional bias against teaching American children about the Holocaust."[51] And New York Representative Stephen J. Solarz testified that: "My district is home to more Holocaust survivors than any other Congressional district in the country. . . . Any discussion of this subject must begin with the premise that the Holocaust is the central existential fact in the history of human civilization. . . . I have been involved in efforts to introduce Holocaust related curricula to the public schools. . . . When we speak of sustaining the lessons and legacies of the Holocaust, we are not speaking of a Republican or Democratic issue, but one of primary importance to all Americans."[52]

Though Shirley Curry had been discreetly transferred to a more obscure Education Department post just two days before the hearings began, she was called on to give testimony before members of Congress. Responding to committee members' exclusive focus on the Holocaust, Curry rejected the allegation of antisemitism while entirely avoiding other equally thorny issues—for example, her alliance with Schlafly, her membership in the Eagle Forum, and her role in promoting New Right ideology within the department. She told the committee:

I want to solemnly affirm that the published innuendo in the *Washington Post* . . . on the very eve of President Reagan's laying the cornerstone for the Holocaust Memorial Museum, that somehow

the Department in general and I in particular have operated from
some anti-Semitic mode in not granting funds . . . is absolutely
absurd. I . . . believe that current and future generations should
know about this unspeakable tragedy. . . .. I do not feel such atro-
cious regimes as the Nazi Party . . . should be presented to students . . . in a sympathetic light. . . . To further document my
genuine dedication to assuring that the sensitive subject of the
Holocaust has its proper place in our schools, I have actively encouraged the U.S. Holocaust Memorial Council to become part of
the NDN.[53]

When Facing History Executive Director Strom was called to
testify, she did her best to provide a more comprehensive picture of
the curriculum and its detractors. Describing the program's case
study approach, she explained: "Facing History *uses* the history of
the Holocaust to educate students and teachers about the meaning
of human dignity, morality, law, citizenship and human behavior
and to help them make connections between history and their own
lives. The lessons provided by this piece of 20th century history
about bigotry, dehumanization, the roots of violence, individual and
collective responsibility are examined to illuminate the role individual citizens have in a democracy to preserve justice."[54] Strom
rebutted Schlafly's allegation that the program induced moral relativism, arguing instead that it advocated "the application of basic
values—good is good and evil is evil—in the complex and challenging situations which characterize life in modern civilization."
She indirectly responded to charges that the program was antiparent, explaining instead that its promotion of critical, independent
thinking encourages teachers to see their students as "active learners" and "stimulates students to examine and re-examine their
assumptions and the assumptions of others so they can make the
type of informed choices necessary for preserving our democratic
institutions."[55] Finally, Strom argued that schools can and must play
a role in eradicating racism and bigotry from society. Drawing from
Facing History's own lesson plans, she quoted the Holocaust sur-

vivor/school principal who had argued, "Reading, writing, and arithmetic are important only if they serve to make our children more humane."[56]

Judging from their response, members of Congress appeared somewhat limited in their understanding of the broader educational, pedagogical, and philosophical picture Strom had presented. Soon after the hearings took place, sixty-six representatives signed a letter to Secretary Cavazos urging him to investigate the Facing History case and hinting at antisemitism behind the NDN decision. Their framing of the problem avoided coming to grips with the New Right's underlying ideological arguments against the program, though these arguments were central to the New Right's campaign against it. Ironically, the narrow construction of the problem put forward by members of Congress may have inadvertently helped Cavazos resolve the problem in the way he did.

After meeting with Schlafly shortly after the elections, Cavazos wrote Representative Weiss: "I want to assure you that I have thoroughly reviewed this matter and have found no evidence of antisemitic bias against the Facing History and Ourselves program. . . . I do not anticipate overturning the decisions made as part of the grants process last year."[57]

National Dissemination Study Group Director Max McConkey responded to Cavazos's remark by yet again trying to put the funding denial in its larger context. He questioned how much the New Right's opposition to the program fundamentally involved antisemitism, and suggested instead that "the real bias was largely anti-inquiry. The program . . . opens up an intellectual dialogue [that] the right wing, especially religious fundamentalists, find terribly frightening."[58] A high-level Education Department official corroborated this view, eerily echoing words that had been uttered by critics of the Rugg social studies textbooks forty-odd years earlier: "There were people, so-called movement conservatives, making decisions at high levels within the Department who felt young people should not be presented with controversial questions which cause them to think."[59]

Such after-the-fact context setting helps to rectify the historical record, but following as it did on the heels of a more limited public discussion, it did little to counter Cavazos's easy out. Even within the confines of this limited discussion, however, Facing History and its allies won several policy victories: the Program Significance Panel was disbanded; a reputable panel of experts was selected for the third NDN review; Curry was removed from her post; and Cavazos, later admitting that the department had acted problematically in its 1988 funding decision, reinstated the History, Geography, and Civics category and monitored future peer reviews.

In October 1989, Facing History and Ourselves at last received a $60,000 dissemination grant, renewable annually for four years. The program would be successful in securing NDN funds throughout this four-year period, and, under the Clinton administration, would be awarded a second, four-year renewable dissemination grant of $72,000.

A Final Note to the Debate: The "Hate America" Crowd

Most public controversies leave long-term scars, regardless of who was found to be at fault and how the controversy was resolved. In December 1990, a full seven years after Schlafly launched the attack against Facing History at the Department of Education hearings, a critique of the program by the late Holocaust scholar Lucy S. Dawidowicz was published in *Commentary*, a conservative Jewish magazine. Readily grasping what Congress had not—that Facing History does not study the Holocaust exclusively but instead uses it as a case study to examine contemporary issues—Dawidowicz reiterated many of Schlafly's arguments and defended the Department of Education against the charge of antisemitism.

In her article, Dawidowicz noted that years earlier, she had declined a request to defend Facing History. "My own reading of the curriculum persuaded me that the Department of Education had ample reason to turn down the grant application," she explained.

"Putatively a curriculum to teach the Holocaust, Facing History was also a vehicle for instructing thirteen-year-olds in civil disobedience and indoctrinating them with propaganda for nuclear disarmament."[60] Like Schlafly, Dawidowicz had never set foot in a Facing History classroom. Her appraisal was based on a review of textual materials and a reading of students' comments about the course— the same comments Schlafly had repeatedly misquoted. From this evidence, Dawidowicz concluded that Facing History promoted pacifism and moral relativism. She charged it and related curricula with offering "exercises in outright political indoctrination in currently fashionable causes" by drawing "parallel[s] between the Holocaust and a potential nuclear holocaust" and by "reflect[ing] the attitudes of the 'hate-America' crowd."[61]

Though Dawidowicz shared many of Schlafly's criticisms of the Facing History program, her opposition was largely fueled by a different concern. Facing History was in fact only one of twenty-five Holocaust education programs she lambasted in her piece. All were faulted for "universalizing" the Holocaust, "deflecting attention from the Jews as the sole or most prominent victims of genocide" by "categorizing this particular crime as an act . . . which can be committed against any people, nation, or race."[62] In voicing this concern, Dawidowicz aligned herself with some Jewish opponents of Facing History who had charged that its "case study" approach undermined the Holocaust's "uniqueness."[63]

Perhaps more to the point for this discussion, Dawidowicz interpreted the effort to universalize genocide as a contemporary response to the pressure of minority groups. Dawidowicz was a member of the board of advisors of the National Association of Scholars (NAS), a group of university professors and other academics founded in the 1980s to defend the traditional canon and to protest the "dogmatic ideology and intellectual intolerance" it argued increasingly "distort[ed]" the academic environment. Since its formation, the NAS has sought to lead the campaign against curricular innovations ranging from multiculturalism to women's studies to social responsibility programs, including moral education.

Many of Dawidowicz's colleagues on the NAS board (among them Irving Kristol, William Kristol's father; Chester E. Finn, Jr.; and conservative Boston University president John R. Silber) have been among the most prominent academic voices criticizing contemporary educational trends. "The banner of cultural diversity is apparently being raised by some whose paramount interest actually lies in attacking the West and its institutions," the NAS proclaimed in a statement concerning bias in the curriculum.[64]

Dawidowicz's complaint against Facing History and Ourselves was in keeping with the New Right and conservative backlash against multicultural and related initiatives, and grounded in the Right's long-standing opposition to what it regarded as moral and cultural relativism. In her article, Dawidowicz argued that

> history is being squeezed out to make room for subject matter demanded by special-interest groups. Blacks have called for teaching about the role of blacks in American history and culture, and Hispanics, Native Americans, and women have followed suit, giving rise to what has irreverently been labeled "oppression studies." The original psychological rationale for these studies—that they would foster pupils' self-esteem—has now been superseded by an ideological rationale which preaches the equality of all cultures and attacks the "hegemony" of Western civilization and its "Eurocentric" character. In either case, the time and space that could be devoted to studying the murder of the European Jews shrink even more.[65]

Commentary published a series of readers' responses to the Dawidowicz piece three months after the original article appeared. Most of these letters shared the author's point of view, though according to FHAO Executive Director Strom, numerous letters in defense of the program never made their way into print. Letters from both Schlafly and NDN reviewer Price appeared in Commentary's pages. Both reiterated their charges against the Facing History program; Price defended her original review of the curriculum, and Schlafly publicly misquoted Facing History's students for a third time.

The *Commentary* article and the letters it elicited received wide distribution. Strom subsequently learned that it was sent out to Holocaust education programs nationwide and to individuals potentially supportive of the Facing History program. The article was also reprinted in *Network News and Views*, a magazine published by the Educational Excellence Network,[66] an organization directed by Chester E. Finn and at one time chaired by Diane Ravitch, the Columbia Teachers College professor who had criticized the New York regents' multicultural guidelines and who later served as an Assistant Secretary of Education under Bush. As a consequence of the article's distribution, negative and distorted portrayals of the Facing History program circulated nationwide. Though Facing History's NDN dissemination funding was not jeopardized, private fundraising efforts were adversely affected, and people potentially interested in the program were warned against it. Thus, some of the criticisms raised publicly in the 1980s continue to haunt Facing History and Ourselves.

Making Sense of the Opposition

The story of the curriculum battle that ensued over Facing History and Ourselves tells us something about educational priorities and policy-making in the Reagan and Bush years. But the way the issues raised by the Facing History and Ourselves story were fought out tells us something more generally about American politics and culture. In many ways, the real issues at stake in the decision to support or oppose FHAO were never adequately addressed. It is possible, perhaps even likely, that had the battle to defend Facing History been waged more explicitly around the issues central to the New Right's critique of the program, the funding decision would have remained the same. But the fact that it was by and large not waged on these grounds is also illuminating and raises an important question. Why was the public debate around the controversy so out of step with Facing History's classroom practice and largely tangential to the real issues at stake—vastly conflicting understandings of education's purpose in American society, indeed conflicting visions of American society, its history, and its future course?

The answer to this question concerns the dominant discourse of American political culture. This discourse posits the existence of a democratic vision that is equally shared by the entire American people, and that equally serves individual Americans regardless of their gender, race, and class. Since certain allegedly agreed-on values are deemed to constitute the "public interest," this normative discourse defines the presumed democratic consensus as being of inherely positive value. It therefore tends to exclude from thought visions not premised on consensus, confining them to the denigrated category of divisive "ideologies." As a result, public discussion of unavoidably political issues is often framed in terms that appeal to certain so-called "shared" democratic values. Though mythic, these values are powerful not because they are simply imposed from above, but because they are produced and reproduced through a hegemonic discourse adhered to by most members of American society.

This is not to suggest that all members of society unquestioningly accept the same construction of the world, or that different life experiences do not influence individual beliefs. In fact, individuals differently positioned in relation to gender, race, ethnicity, or class may hold different (and conflicting) interpretations of the same experiences and events, and the perspectives of particular individuals may be shaped by multiple, and at times even contradictory, identities. Nor is it to suggest that mythic content remains unchanged over time, or that the terms of this discourse are not the object of social and political struggle. As the history of educational debates over moral education makes clear, opposing viewpoints on American society translate into conflicts over public policy in a number of realms, including education.

Finally, I suggest not that cultural values are uniform or arbitrary, but that dominant narratives reflect and serve dominant interests, and that all members of a society are, in some form or other, enveloped within a culture's mythic discourse. These values include a belief in individual agency and in the equation of individual progress with the public good; a belief in freedom, equality, and opportunity for all; a belief in the glory of a revolutionary past and in the promise of an even brighter future. These values are reflected in the concept of a pluralist democracy and presumed to operate through political mechanisms that admit diversity yet benefit all. For example, all citizens can elect representatives who will defend their interests; these representatives can exert pressure to hold officials accountable; society is made up of groups that bring together diverse interests; all individuals belong to these groups; and all groups are equally heard.

The prevailing pluralist discourse is both descriptive and ideological, expressing a belief in how politics *does* work and in how it *should* work. Though it acknowledges diversity within the American social body, it obscures real differences in power relations by appealing to consensual values. Though it acknowledges gaps between present imperfections and democratic ideals, it represents these gaps as areas where self-improvement can occur, appealing to the limitless potential of the individual to bring America's promise into being. The dominant political discourse both elicits and absorbs social criticism, rendering it difficult to identify and struggle over genuine political differences, and nearly impossible to contest or extend the boundaries of the prevailing definition of democracy. Within this context, we can review the roles of various players within the Facing History funding controversy and make sense of the terms in which the debate was posed.

The media's narrow focus on antisemitism within the Facing History public story is neither surprising nor atypical. The word *Nazi* makes for easy headlines. The newspapers' angle on the story provided dramatic, albeit limited, coverage of a complex story. But it was also in keeping with the prevailing cultural tendency—often reflected and furthered by the media—to avoid confronting the substantive issues at stake, and to portray controversy in simple terms of "good guys" and "bad guys" rather than probe the issues that underlie political struggle. The coverage of the Facing History debacle is only one of numerous instances in which the media has distorted—or worse yet, inflamed—controversial educational issues, impoverishing the public's fuller understanding of the problem.

A dramatic recent example of such reporting can be seen in the uproar created in 1992 when then–New York City Chancellor of Education Joseph A. Fernandez endorsed the multicultural "Children of the Rainbow" curriculum, which included among its over 600-book bibliography three picture books for young children encouraging a tolerant attitude toward homosexuals. Though Pat Robertson's Christian Coalition and other New Right groups can be credited with organizing local parents to oppose the books and the curriculum itself, the media's sensationalizing of the controversy helped fan the flames of homophobia and, according to the ousted chancellor, convinced "lots of the people in the middle" to adopt the New Right's point of view. As with the Facing History case, citizens were effectively denied the means to make judgments that should not only have been more informed, but also more complex and nuanced.[67]

Members of Congress adopted the media's sensational and narrow framing of the Facing History story, whether because of their incomplete understanding, their electoral concerns, or both. They posed the problem in terms of a social taboo. Antisemitism is not culturally acceptable (not publicly, anyway), and when framed within the context of Republican wrongdoing, the issue could potentially be turned to political advantage. At the same time, Republican and Democratic leaders appeal to the same pluralist vision to argue their case.

In dealing with the media and in testimony before Congress, the Facing History organization repeatedly attempted to present an accurate, multifaceted picture of its curriculum and a more thorough, far-reaching analysis of the program's opposition. But for the most part, their efforts went unheard, and the group ultimately resigned itself to making the most of congressional support and media attention, however narrowly framed. In September 1988, Executive Director Strom wrote letters to prominent journalists suggesting possible connections between the program's funding denial and the discovery of Bush campaign consultants with an antisemitic past. Strom also sent a letter to key members of the House and Senate that emphasized the course's Holocaust focus rather than its more fundamental intention to promote critical thinking, multicultural tolerance, and social responsibility. "I attended the Cornerstone Dedication Ceremony at the U.S. Holocaust Memorial Museum last week, when I heard President Reagan speak about those who would obstruct and deny the history of the Holocaust," she wrote. "I was struck by the irony that funding for a nationally acclaimed 'blue-ribbon' education program on the Holocaust . . . was turned down by the U.S. Department of Education for a third time."

Strom's actions in no way signify a shift in her thinking about the central purpose of the curriculum. Instead, they seem to have reflected a political assessment of the dimension of the program most newsworthy and most likely to win congressional support. Caught within the politics of the policy process, the Facing History organization eventually argued its cause in terms somewhat tangential to its broader pedagogical purpose. Ironically, a curriculum that some Jewish groups had criticized for "universalizing the Holocaust" defended itself by staking out Holocaust territory.

Though the organization's decision may well have been tactically sound, it also signifies something more problematic: an appeal to an allegedly neutral notion of democracy, a disinclination to define its educational endeavor in political terms, and an unwillingness to acknowledge that the values it espouses have the potential to challenge the powers that be. Advocates of the Facing History program condemn injustice in contemporary society and consider education an instrument for redressing it. But in keeping with a discourse that simultaneously invites and thwarts social dissent, Facing History accepts the terms of a mythic "American way" rather than problematizing it. This at times ambiguous position has ramifications for classroom practice, as we saw earlier in classroom discussions where thorny political issues were debated.

Schlafly and her New Right colleagues partake of some aspects of the normative discourse and conflict with others. In arguing that her construction of "what should be taught in American schools" is apolitical, Schlafly allies herself with the allegedly neutral democratic consensus. But in articulating her absolutist understanding of behavior, morality, and patriotism as *the*—not *a*—cultural truth, she runs headfirst into liberal pluralism. The New Right's political project thus enjoys a strong and solid base that gives it political clout, but it also faces hostility and rejection by those who adhere to a more "culturally tolerant" democratic vision.

It is typical of American political culture that issues as complicated and important as these often get fought out in veiled terms. Rarely are the underlying conflicts about values, social goals, and conceptions of American identity brought to the surface and debated explicitly and thoroughly. Rarer still are they democratically resolved.

Chapter Seven

Conclusion:
Educating for Democracy

> To guarantee maximum understanding, the very
> foundation of education must be the study of the
> actual problems and controversial issues of our
> people. There is no way by which the democratic
> principle of consent can be carried on other than that
> of the parliamentary discussion of issues. But consent
> based upon knowledge of only one aspect or side of a
> problem, upon the avoidance of controversy, is a
> travesty of both knowledge and democracy. To keep
> issues out of the school, therefore, is to keep thought
> out of it; it is to keep life out of it.
> —*Harold Rugg,* That Men May Understand, 1941

On February 8, 1994, the Education and Labor Committee of the
U.S. House of Representatives voted 23 to 6 to defeat an amendment calling for a national conference and demonstration grants to
further the teaching of values like honesty, kindness, responsibility,
and integrity in America's public schools. This marked the seventh
time since 1987 that a character education amendment had failed
to work its way through Congress and become law.[1] Opposition to
the amendment crossed party lines, a sign of how nervous lawmakers are when it comes to the question of values education in
America's public schools.

As we have already seen, conservatives have often alleged that
school-based programs seeking to promote moral values indoctri-

nate students with views that are liberal and "politically correct," alienating children from their parents' own moral priorities and beliefs. But liberal politicians have at times been equally distrustful, seeing values education as a means by which New Right activists are trying to insinuate their own religious and political beliefs into public education. As a consequence of these fears and suspicions, an interesting disjuncture is developing between grassroots activity and policy-making. On the one hand, lawmakers and government officials have been reluctant to become involved in initiatives where values education is explicitly addressed and promoted. On the other hand, a groundswell of moral education activity is building in public schools across the country. Schools are increasingly seeking to fight diverse social problems—including violence, sexual abuse, the alleged breakdown of the family, and growing disparities between rich and poor—with a variety of values-oriented approaches. These may promote a specific "value of the month" for students to live up to, for example, or they may recognize and affirm students' daily moral acts within the school community.[2] Though many of these initiatives differ significantly from Facing History's focus on interweaving moral lessons into the study of history, they share that program's premise that schools have a vital role to play in nurturing the moral growth of the young. As a result, these newer initiatives have at times faced opposition and controversy similar to what Facing History and Ourselves encountered in the 1980s.

Reframing the Debate

One way to make sense of the debates about moral education in the public schools and to assess the place of moral education in American politics and culture is to pose three fundamental and overlapping questions: What should our schools be teaching? How should they be teaching it? Who are they teaching it to? I will address each of these questions in turn, bringing interpretations of classroom practice to bear on some of the key issues at stake. In doing so, I will suggest that these debates about moral education have not always been useful in helping us understand what actually goes on in the classroom or in determining how we can best educate students and meet their various needs. It does not get us very far, for example, to cast "basics" and "values" as binary opposites; nor is it useful to insist that any departure from indoctrinating pedagogy will inevitably lead to moral relativism. I think that we should dispense with sterile dichotomies and reframe some of the issues in order to think more clearly about what we need to do in the classroom. Such reframing may help us understand the different ways diverse people approach these contentious issues, and it may also further our thinking on what American education should be about.

What Should Schools Teach?

Those who argue over what public schools should teach are concerned with many issues, but perhaps chief among them is the place of "basics" in the school curriculum. Generally speaking, conservative and New Right critics tend to counterpose teaching educational basics to promoting critical moral thinking. They see the two as competing for the precious few hours in the school day. And, perhaps implicitly, they suggest that the two endeavors are conceptually at odds. If students spend time interpreting their own beliefs and preoccupying themselves with difficult moral dilemmas, the thinking goes, they may be unable to focus on more traditional content areas. New Right activist Phyllis Schlafly argued these points in her criticism of Facing History and Ourselves and similar programs during the Department of Education "ethical responsibility" hearings and in her later lobbying of William Kristol. And some aspects of these arguments have been put forward by more moderate critics, like E. D. Hirsch, Jr., in his controversial work *Cultural Literacy: What Every American Needs to Know*.[3] Similar charges were leveled in the 1950s against the legacy of Progressive educational reforms.

Conservatives and New Right activists are not alone in worrying that basic subjects are getting short shrift, however. Many parents who would never align themselves with the New Right's political project decry today's allegedly declining educational standards. Even President Clinton's Deputy Secretary of Education Madeleine Kunin seems to regard teaching moral values as something quite distinct from basic educational subject matter. In telling a reporter from the *Wall Street Journal* why she had declined a briefing on character education from the Character Education Partnership, a nonprofit organization "dedicated to developing moral character and civic virtue" in young people, she explained that she found the subject "interesting" but perhaps "inappropriate" for federal involvement. "Our focus is on academics. That's where we see our most urgent needs."[4]

The school day *is* short, though students may not always experience it that way, and a legitimate argument can be made against programs that divorce critical moral lessons from other aspects of school learning. The values clarification approach that was so popular in the 1960s and 1970s may merit criticism on these grounds. But it seems to me that we create a false dichotomy when we *necessarily* counterpose "basics" and "moral learning," for moral issues are embedded in most aspects of the school's "basic" subject matter—and certainly in every work of literature students read and in every period of history they study. Political conservatives like President Reagan's Secretary of Education William Bennett believe that moral lessons should be grounded within traditional content areas; in fact, some of the allegedly "liberal" curricula that Bennett and his colleagues oppose do just that.[5]

Portraits of how the Facing History and Ourselves program is actually taught in the classroom provide many examples of an almost seamless integration of history lessons and a more personal exploration of key moral, social, and political issues. We glimpsed many of these portraits earlier in the book, as I described the implementation of the program at the Medgar Evers school. In class sessions where students discussed religious beliefs, for example, they learned about polytheism and monotheism, the Christian roots of antisemitism, and religious and cultural practices in Europe in the 1500s. At the same time, they engaged in both public and private reflection on their own religious beliefs, and on their own attitudes and actions toward people who believed, looked, or acted differently from themselves. When contentious political differences were brought to the surface later on in the course, students discussed, among other things, the notorious Dreyfus Affair that erupted in France in the 1890s, the origins of the state system in the Middle East dating back to the post–World War I period, and the ways the Ku Klux Klan organized and promoted its beliefs in the 1970s. Again, interwoven throughout these discussions were students' personal reflections on how individuals—in the political arena as well as the classroom—can ethically and productively respond to the expression of controversial or offensive ideas in the public arena.

As I see it, students' understanding of history was reinforced rather than diminished by their simultaneous engagement with complex moral, social, and political issues in these class sessions. At the same time, the classes enhanced students' use of the essential learning skills of reading, writing, listening, and oral expression, as well as their use of higher-order thinking processes in integrating various domains of knowledge. After observing these and many other classes and speaking with students at length, it seems to me both foolish and wasteful to try to divorce the moral issues necessarily embedded in every aspect of students' learning from the particular subject matter they happen to explore, or to deprive students of a guided space in which they can wrestle with moral questions raised by the material they confront. Pitting critical moral learning against educational basics is a false dichotomy. The question seems to me not *whether* teachers should help draw out moral lessons from students' engagement with basic content area, but rather *how* they should attempt to do so—a question to which we will turn in a moment.

A parallel concern regarding the content of the curriculum is whether schools should even allow, much less invite, discussion of contemporary moral, social, and political issues in the classroom.

Many conservative and New Right activists argue that they should not. They hold that schools are—or at least should be—apolitical environments, and thus should not be in the business of encouraging students to engage with potentially divisive issues that are being fought over in society at large. This concern fuels at least some of the recent attacks against multiculturalism and so-called "political correctness." Some have argued that certain multicultural programs may actually distort historical "truths." (By the same token, of course, one could also argue that the more traditional Eurocentric version of things has surely provided its own distorted lens.) It has also been argued that the climate of "political correctness" that allegedly dominates America's schools, colleges, and universities restricts students' freedom of expression, forcing them into an ideological straightjacket of conformism to a liberal or even radical agenda.

But I would argue that a good deal of the energy behind critics' attacks is generated not so much by "political correctness" and multiculturalism in and of themselves, but by the broader social changes that these tendencies reflect and that critics find frightening. These include shifts in the ethnic makeup of the American population and the new questions these shifts provoke about how American culture should be defined. They also concern changes in gender roles, especially the roles of women in society, and the consequent reshuffling of gender relations in both the public and private realms. These are contentious issues in American society, and many feel uncomfortable with the idea of young people grappling with them. Underpinning much of the feeling that controversial issues should be kept out of the schools lies the anxiety that moral, social, or political discussions in school may lead young people away from the beliefs of their parents, church, or community. Competing ideas about who is in fact responsible for the moral upbringing of the young—parents, religious institutions, schools, the government, or some combination of these—underlie these concerns. Articulating the perspective voiced by those on the New Right in their opposition to Facing History and Ourselves and similar values-oriented curricula, conservative Texas Republican Richard Armey argued to members of the House Education and Labor Committee during the character education amendment debate: "I for one would not tolerate anybody having the presumption to dare to think they should define who my children are, what their values are, what their ethics are and who in the hell they will be in this world. The fact is these people don't know my children and the fact is they don't love my children. And the fact is they don't care about my children and the further fact is they accept no responsibility for the outcome . . . and they ought to, by God, leave my kids alone."[6]

But it is not only New Right activists who are concerned about schools undermining parental authority. Many parents who regard themselves as moderates or liberals may also worry about what is being taught in the classroom and how it affects their role as parents. The fact that the media has often sensationalized conflicts over what goes on behind school walls has not made things any easier for parents in this regard.[7]

Conflicts over the dangers or benefits of engaging students in discussion of controversial issues stretches back at least half a century, to the turmoil catalyzed by Harold Rugg's deliberate attempt to stimulate critical dialogue through his social studies texts. These conflicts have persisted through the decades, surfacing, for example, in the New Right's assault on Facing History in the 1980s, and more recently still in the crisis over the "Rainbow curriculum" in New York City. In 1993, the New York City Board of Education voted to remove Chancellor Joseph A. Fernandez because of his support for initiatives that included AIDS education, condom distribution, and a curriculum that advocated tolerance for diverse social groups, including homosexuals. According to Carol Ann Gresser, the board's chair, parents were upset by Fernandez's promotion of a "social agenda" in the schools. "You can't bring into the classroom issues that haven't even been decided by the society," she said.[8]

I would argue exactly the opposite: one cannot avoid bringing into the classroom issues over which society is still divided, because students themselves are well aware of these issues and hungry to discuss them with their peers; they need and want help in learning how to do so. Complex moral issues are as much a part of the "hidden curriculum" of the school day—the countless interactions between students and their teacher in classrooms and on the playground—as they are embedded in the basic content areas students explore.[9] That these moral issues will at times rub up against sensitive political issues and debates is unavoidable.

The students in this book may again serve as testimony to this fact. For it was Chi-Ho who inadvertently catalyzed a discussion about present-day antisemitism by suggesting that an international Jewish conspiracy might, in fact, exist. It was Abby who propelled her teachers and classmates into a discussion of Israeli policy toward Palestinians, past and present. And as I described at the beginning of this book, it was a group of students from Dorchester, Massachusetts, who performed a skit critical of police searches at the Massachusetts Civil Liberties Union's Rap Against Racism, protesting what they saw as racist police practices in the city of Boston. The liveliness of these various episodes speaks to students' passionate investment in controversial moral, social, and political issues. Arguing in favor of keeping these issues out of the classroom is at the very least futile, since it seems they will inevitably make their way in. A more fruitful discussion might focus on how these issues should be taught.

How Should Schools Teach?

Pedagogical questions divide those who support bringing moral issues into the schoolroom. Some favor traditional approaches that *indoctrinate* young people with particular moral beliefs about right and wrong. Others seek to stimulate students' own *critical moral reasoning* and *judgment*. Advocates of indoctrinating methods can lay claim to a rich heritage. Harking back to the early days of public schooling, they note that American schools have long sought to instill virtues considered essential to democratic citizenship—

among them honesty, thrift, promptness, hard work, and patriotism. Until the era of Progressive education reforms, these values were explicitly conveyed through discipline, moral example, and curricular subject matter. Stories in the *McGuffey Reader*—a text that, by 1919, was second only to the Bible in circulation—provided children with countless moral examples of the "good" and "right" way to behave.[10]

Some of today's educational conservatives—for example, former Education Secretary William Bennett and University of Illinois professor of education Edward Wynne—call for a renewed focus on the development of moral habits in young people. Against the current of much moral education practice in the past several decades, they argue that traditional approaches are the best way to get there. As moral developmental psychologist William Damon puts it, for Wynne "indoctrination should cease being a dirty word in the educational community."[11] Both Bennett and Wynne value the practice of moral conduct over the acquisition of moral reasoning skills. Wynne tends to focus on the school environment rather than the individual child. His work identifies schools that seek to develop good moral character in students, defined "in a rather traditional fashion" as "not hurting others—observing discipline; and going out of one's way to be polite, truthful, and helpful to others."[12] In a mode antithetical to the individual-oriented values clarification approach, Wynne's work values school activities that further cohesiveness and collaboration—extracurricular groups and clubs, the use of school mottoes, symbols, pep rallies, and other vehicles for developing the values of group loyalty and cooperation. Though he recognizes that developing students' own moral reasoning may be important, he sees this project as secondary to training students in good moral conduct, through discipline and reward.

Bennett shares Wynne's positive view of indoctrinating methods, but he goes further than Wynne in opposing the alternative. Bennett is strongly in favor of emphasizing moral action over thinking; he sees the exercise of moral reflection as inimical to practicing good moral habits. He holds that critical moral reasoning approaches separate moral lessons from their natural contexts; this is why he argues for embedding moral lessons in the schools' traditional content area. He faults critical moral reasoning for its "problem-solving" orientation. The same argument was voiced by New Right critics throughout the 1970s and 1980s, when they objected to programs that allegedly caused students to suffer mental "disequilibrium" by engaging them in discussion of moral dilemmas. "[Schools] would be better off paying attention to old-fashioned character building and simply telling students that certain behavior is wrong,"[13] the Eagle Forum's *Education Reporter* concluded in October 1988. The *Education Reporter* echoed Bennett's claim a few years earlier that

> the [moral] problematic approach denies the most important part of morality, which is not the development of decision-making capacities, but the development of what used to be called . . . character— that is, dispositions and habits of the mind and heart. A moral educationist's model moral person is one who is always in doubt, in dilemma, tearing his hair out, trying to get clear about what to do. The moral individual, however, is rarely presented as a conscientious person, a person of character and equanimity, who, because of his character, doesn't have to face hard decisions every ten minutes or every ten days.[14]

Those committed to stimulating complex moral reasoning and judgment in students would no doubt take issue with this characterization. The cognitive-developmental approach, grounded in the work of Dewey and Piaget, refined and put into practice by Kohlberg, and later implemented in a modified form by Facing History and Ourselves, helps students recognize, discuss, reflect on, and judge conflicting moral claims. Advocates of critical moral reasoning share Bennett and Wynne's desire to produce young people willing and able to act in morally responsible ways. But unlike their critics, they see students' practice of critical moral reasoning as essential to their eventual practice of socially responsible moral acts.

As Facing History Executive Director Margot Stern Strom said when commenting on the outcome of her own program, "the action *is* the thinking."

This does not mean that students must continually be angst-ridden and depressed as they grapple with the moral complexity of the world. But it does mean that they will be encouraged to develop a critical attitude toward almost every aspect of learning—from their interactions on the playground to their discussions with peers in the classroom to their analyses of curricular texts. This critical attitude is seen as essential to developing students' internal "ownership" of what is morally right and wrong. Such an attitude is unlikely to be achieved by Bennett's more externally driven alternative: uncritical absorption of a singular moral perspective.

Other issues also divide those who promote critical moral thinking and indoctrination. There is the concern that parental authority will be undermined if young people are encouraged to develop their own critical moral judgment—a concern Schlafly dubbed "*the* civil rights issue of the 1980s."[15] There is the question of how young people learn best—through direct, personal engagement with subject matter, as Dewey and many of the heirs of the Progressive legacy believe, or through memorization and rote learning, as more traditional educators have argued. There is the conflict over who young people actually are and what they need psychologically and can tolerate, ranging from the cognitive developmentalists' belief that students benefit from directed engagement with complex social issues to the New Right's perception that such engagement qualifies as "child abuse." And there is the perception that in doing away with a singular definition of moral right and wrong and putting independent critical moral thinking in its place, young people will be led to embrace moral relativism.

This last charge was directed against the Facing History and Ourselves curriculum in the 1980s, but it dates further back, to the New Right's general opposition to "secular humanism." In recent years, this charge has been repeated in one form or another, surfacing in Bloom's scathing critique of "moral openness" and in fears voiced by critics of multiculturalism that teaching about the values of diverse cultures will necessarily relativize the values of the West. Perhaps the radical values neutrality proffered by the now almost entirely defunct values clarification method gave some credence to the concern about moral relativism. But it seems to me that some middle ground exists between the poles of moral indoctrination and moral neutrality. In that middle ground, students are involved in discussion of complex moral issues with their peers under the guidance of trained individuals willing to make their own moral perspectives clear.[16] It provides parameters for what constitutes moral thought and action by stressing students' need to respectfully examine a variety of perspectives on issues, helping students to put themselves in another's shoes and to listen to differing, at times conflicting, points of view. Though it seeks to stimulate students' independent moral reasoning, it also requires them to make moral judgments on conflicting claims rather than assign equal merit to all points of view. It provides students with many examples of moral behavior and action—through discussion with or about moral mentors (be they teachers, outside speakers, or peers) and through analysis of curricular materials such as history lessons or fictional stories. Finally, it seeks to reinforce moral lessons that arise in the curriculum within the broader culture of the school as a whole. I believe Facing History's classroom practice provides many instances that this important middle ground exists and can be built on.

Of the various classes I observed throughout the semester, those devoted to exploring questions of religious difference might serve as the best example of this middle ground. In the classes I described in Chapter Three, a fictional story about religious prejudice in the sixteenth century catalyzed students' multifaceted discussion about their own religious beliefs and attitudes. Though students held beliefs that were sometimes widely divergent, they listened to each other in a spirit of respect promoted by classroom teachers. New Right activists, particularly those on the religious Right, might take a different view of these same class episodes, faulting the Facing History program for allowing a discussion of religious belief into the classroom in the first place. After all, the courts have deemed religious instruction inappropriate for America's public schools.

Critics might also condemn the stance taken by teachers throughout these class sessions—that, as teacher Steve Cohen put it, the program will not "tell you this faith is right and this faith is wrong. Nobody can argue that *your* belief in God is any better or worse than anyone else's belief in God. That's something to think about." This stance might be interpreted as an example of "secular humanism," something the Right has defined as itself a religion. The fact that students expressed a variety of religious perspectives throughout the classes I observed, that diverse perspectives received equal consideration and respect, and that students were challenged to regard their own beliefs as contingent (again Steve Cohen: "I suspect that through this course you're going to look again and again at the things you believe in and ask yourself, 'Why *do* I believe in that?'") might well validate critics' worst fears. These, as we have seen, include the fears that the program undermines parental authority, invades students' psychological privacy, and violates the authority of divinely inspired absolute truth.

I tend to look at these class sessions differently. Instead of moral relativism, I see an effort to communicate several key values: a consistent regard for the importance of religious belief in giving meaning to peoples' lives across diverse cultures and time periods; an insistence that students recognize the importance of religious "truths" in each others' experience, even if these truths conflict with their own; a commitment to helping students listen to one another; and a refusal to tolerate any disrespect for beliefs different from their own.

I would argue that as a result of the consistent transmission of these important values, students were able to engage in a fruitful discussion with their peers. This is true despite the fact that the religious beliefs expressed in class ranged from a devout Christian faith to an equally "devout" adherence to atheism. So, too, did students' learning seem to take place on levels of increasing cognitive complexity, beginning with their grasp of specific historical content, building toward a more sophisticated ability to link historical study with personal exploration, and eventually leading (through out-of-class journal assignments) to an ability to extend in-class learning to life outside the classroom.

An astute observation by Josh, one of Facing History's more verbal students, suggests that the program has been successful in conveying to students that common values may unite us despite our differences. "I could be wrong," he says tentatively, "but I think that with the stories in any religion's bible, it's not that they're true or false, it's the *values* behind them that matter." While some of Josh's classmates seemed a bit uncomfortable sorting through the multiple points of view expressed in class, Josh's own remark suggests that he and perhaps others were able to hear and integrate diverse perspectives.

This brings us to a final question of contention: Who in fact are the students we are teaching? What are their capabilities and needs, and how can we help them best?

Who Are Schools Teaching?

Two radically different views of young people inform many of the views on education that I have discussed in this book. One view, advanced by New Right activists, conservative educators, and some concerned parents, depicts young people as being innocent and in need of protection. From this perspective, subjecting them to controversial political and social issues and compelling them to sort through conflicting moral claims is psychologically damaging. Schools therefore have a responsibility to safeguard young people from potentially disturbing and deleterious subject matter. Those who adhere to this view have not always clearly articulated what age groups they are speaking about, but their opposition to numerous curricula used in middle and high school settings suggests that adolescents are included in their definition of the children who should be protected from such programs.

Cognitive developmentalists put forward a different view.

Following Piaget's schema, they regard adolescence as a turning point in cognitive development, marked by the child's ability to reason abstractly for the first time. Psychologists like Lawrence Kohlberg and Carol Gilligan, and educational practitioners like the teachers in the Facing History and Ourselves program, seek to nurture this shift in intellectual and psychological development. Engaging students in discussions of complex moral dilemmas, fostering their ability to listen to alternative perspectives, and supporting their nascent attempts to reflect critically on their own moral beliefs are seen as steps conducive to nurturing such growth.

Such opposing views of adolescent development lead us to ask an obvious but too often ignored question: What is the view from inside the classroom?

I believe students in the Facing History classroom were, at times, angered, troubled, and perplexed by the moral dilemmas and divergent views they encountered in class. For example, toward the end of the course, students were clearly uncomfortable when contentious political differences were aired about such topics as freedom of speech and the Arab-Israeli conflict. The friendship between Chi-Ho and Josh was strained when Chi-Ho voiced antisemitic beliefs; relations were similarly strained between Abby and Sandra when Abby's views on the Middle East struck Sandra as misguided; and the values of both Abby's and Josh's parents were implicitly called into question. Angered and hurt, some students retreated into simplistic, either-or thinking: both Josh and Sandra demanded to be told "what is true" in order to settle their personal scores. Such discomfort provides grist for those who perceive students as incapable of handling complexity and who see conflict itself as necessarily unproductive.

In my opinion, however, these same Facing History students were wonderfully involved in class sessions, and indeed quite ready, eager, and able to deal with the controversies aroused. Though some of the teachers' contributions to these discussions were partisan and, from my perspective, problematic, I nonetheless valued their ability to facilitate discussion among members of the class, helping students reexamine their own assumptions and listen to each other despite their anger. Thus, though Sandra begged for closure, she tolerated not getting it; though Josh demanded to be separated from Chi-Ho, he continued to sit next to his friend; though Marysa opposed Abby, she engaged her in open debate; and though Abby felt intimidated, she stood her ground. In short, while tempers were high, feelings impassioned, and intellects fiercely engaged, the group never closed down or fell apart. In the class sessions, students seemed to me terrifically stimulated by the powerful emotions unleashed by contentious debates. My later interviews bore out that the conflicts students took part in energized them rather than leaving them overwhelmed and disheartened. They certainly left class feeling anything other than apathetic.

A second issue in determining who we are teaching concerns how we believe students "take in" what they are taught. Advocates of traditional top-down pedagogical methods implicitly believe that students uncritically internalize what is handed down to them. Of course, those who accept this notion of education may be unhappy about the consequences, depending on what specific moral or political message they believe is being inculcated.

My own observations find students both less permeable and more resilient. For example, students at the Massachusetts Civil Liberties Union's Rap About Racism came to the event with their own deeply rooted racial attitudes, and these attitudes influenced how they interpreted what transpired at the conference that day. Facing History's middle school students came to class similarly positioned—conscious of some of their own beliefs and attitudes and ready to defend them. Thus, early on in the course, some boys publicly took issue with a curricular resource film's negative portrayal of hunting, and toward the end of the semester, Abby steadfastly stood her ground against the traditional civil liberties argument for free speech.

The ability of students to persevere in the midst of struggle, and to resist (or at the very least, to reflect critically on) what they hear, implies that they are not passive consumers of whatever moral or political perspectives they encounter. Instead, these twelve- and thirteen-year-olds seem to sift and sort through what they are presented with, rejecting some of it and adopting some of it while wrestling with themselves, their peers, and their teachers along the way. This finding undermines Schlafly's view of the child, and more broadly, the warnings of all those concerned about the allegedly damaging effects of critical moral education, multiculturalism, and "politically correct" thinking in the schools. But it may also cast doubt on the promise of educators within the values education movement who argue, perhaps too optimistically at times, that students will eventually adopt the prosocial values and behaviors presented in class.

I will mention another aspect of the question of who students are only briefly. This concerns the composition of the classroom: How diverse or homogeneous is our public school student body? Do multicultural curricula "fracture" the cohesiveness of the classroom (and by extension, the greater community), or do they reflect who actually sits there? Do discussions about sexuality promote homosexuality, or do they help students realize that diverse sexual preferences exist? Do discussions of religious differences raise the specter of multiple religious truths, or do they reflect what students know and who they are in the first place?

The students in the public school classroom I observed were a diverse group: black, white, Latino, Asian; boys and girls; gay and straight; Jewish, Protestant, Catholic, atheist. They came into the classroom well aware of some, but not all, of their differences. Sitting together in an urban public school classroom in the Northeast, the ethnic diversity of this class was perhaps atypical only to the extent that it included as many white faces as it did. A full forty years after the Brown v. Board of Education decision, America's public schools are still largely segregated, de facto rather than de jure, and our urban schools are increasingly repositories for students of color. The twelve- and thirteen-year-olds in this multiracial classroom were clearly aware of and exposed to diverse social problems beyond school walls. Already differently positioned in relation to these problems at the beginning of the school year, they became even more conscious of their differences as the semester went on.

So the question is: How can the content of what we teach and the manner in which we teach it enable students like these to interact productively once they leave the school environment? What can we do to best prepare them for their role as future citizens?

Struggling Over American Values

Debates about what American public schools should teach, how they should teach it, and who they are teaching it to have always been tied to conflicting visions of American democracy and its future. Residents of Lake County, Florida, near Orlando, are learning this lesson well. In 1992, the State of Florida enacted a law mandating multicultural education. In May 1994, the three fundamentalist Christian members on Lake County's five-person school board voted to adopt a resolution requiring teachers to promote the idea that America is unquestionably superior to any other society in all of human history.[17] The resolution specifically mandates instilling in students "an appreciation of . . . our republican form of government, capitalism, a free-enterprise system, patriotism, strong family values, freedom of religion, and other basic values that are superior to other foreign or historical cultures."[18]

The school board's decision quickly attracted national media attention. It was hailed by conservative syndicated columnist Patrick Buchanan and ridiculed by *New York Times* columnist Anna Quindlen. It inspired a member of a community school board in Queens, New York, to propose a similarly worded resolution.[19] In Lake County itself, the resolution led angry citizens to form groups like "People for Mainstream Values" to protest and reverse the school board's decision. A Florida teachers' union affiliated with the American Federation of Teachers announced its intention to challenge the policy in court, arguing that it violated the state's requirement that schools should seek to "eliminate personal and national ethnocentrism so that [students] understand that a specific culture is not intrinsically superior or inferior to another."[20]

The school board majority's controversial "America first" stance is only one of many battles initiated by its chair, Pat Hart, a member of the Christian Coalition. Hart's previous campaigns have included refusing Head Start money, limiting sex education, banning certain reading material, and mandating the inclusion of creationism in the science curriculum. Local battles like these have taken place all across the country in recent years, usually spearheaded by New Right activists intent on reclaiming America's public schools from what they perceive to be liberal domination.[21] But things do not always seem so clear-cut to people on the ground—including some of the Lake County teachers who will be called on to implement the new policy. "We need clearer definitions," complained a social studies teacher responsible for teaching American history. "We regard American culture as very diverse, and we're not sure what values they see as American culture."[22]

Throughout American history, there have been contentious debates about which values are authentically and truly "American." This has been the case even though, with rare exceptions, those engaged in these debates have sought to bolster their own version of these values by defining them as authentically and eternally "American," and thus nonideological and even nonpolitical. Though at different points on the political spectrum, both Phyllis Schlafly and Facing History and Ourselves have at times appealed to allegedly neutral, transcendent democratic ideals to support their own agenda for America's public schools. But the history of debates over American education demonstrates that so-called American values are not, never have been, and never can be politically neutral. Supporters of one curriculum or another may use the same words (*freedom, democracy, justice,* and so on), but they often have different understandings of what these words mean. Those different understandings may translate into different interpretations of what goes on in the classroom: what one observer may see as an informed, active, participatory debate in a critical moral thinking classroom may be perceived by a critic as unruly, disrespectful, anxiety-provoking, and unproductive chaos.

These differences are not epiphenomenal or transitory. They reflect the inescapable fact that the United States is an extremely heterogeneous society, comprising diverse (but overlapping) subgroups defined by racial, gender, class, ethnic, religious, political, and other characteristics. Individuals and groups see themselves as having certain social interests and goals, and they seek to achieve them through the political process. Even when some seemingly obvious material interest is involved, those who seek to satisfy this interest generally see themselves as motivated by lofty ideals. It should therefore come as no surprise that our society is ridden by conflicts, and that those conflicts are often fought out in terms of conflicting visions of history, of who we are as a society, and of where we are (and should be) going. Indeed, in the liberal democratic political theory on which this country's system of government is based, it is precisely the purpose and role of government to provide mechanisms whereby conflicting interests can be accommodated, reconciled, and at least partially satisfied through bargaining and compromise.

Of course, this is not how the system has always worked in practice, and it is not exactly how it operates even today. When the Constitution was drawn up certain groups were deliberately excluded from political participation, most notably blacks and women, and it took some time before even poor white males were fully enfranchised. Even today, there are privileged elements and institutions in American society that, thanks to their wealth or position or connections, exercise a greatly disproportionate influence on the political process. At the same time, it is important to keep in mind that throughout American history, disenfranchised and subordinated groups have struggled, in alliance with others, to compel America to live up to its professed ideals by incorporating them into the body politic on equal terms. And campaigns to deepen and extend the rights and constitutional protections that Americans enjoy have also been a constant theme in this country's history. Such struggles continue in our own day as well, of course, and will go on in the future; they too are part of what democracy is about.

It is precisely because democracy is still a goal to be attained, is a work in progress, that what goes on in our public schools is so important. Those schools can, should, and must be an arena in which future citizens are prepared to deal with contentious issues and learn to make the kinds of moral choices adults are constantly called on to make. I would suggest that what a critical moral education program like Facing History and Ourselves is doing is preparing students to meet this important challenge. This does not mean an effort to instill in young people a fixed set of beliefs about what is "right" and "wrong" or "good" and "bad." It means helping them acquire certain democratic predispositions and habits of mind in as informed and responsible a way as possible. The capacity to listen to other people's beliefs and perspectives, and to reflect on them critically, is a crucial starting point in this process. Approaches to values education that try to avoid all moral constraints are certainly counterproductive, but using indoctrination to implant a capacity for informed moral choice is at least equally counterproductive.

Political philosopher Amy Gutmann has advanced a similar vision of the purpose of public education in a democratic society. She argues that it should be grounded in a commitment to what she calls "conscious social reproduction"—the project of "collectively re-creating the society that we share."[23] Gutmann has usefully suggested that to help young people critically evaluate the conflictual issues they will encounter as citizens, public education must be informed by two fundamental principles that will act as constraints on the authority of parents and the state. The first is *nonrepression*, which "prevents the state, and any group within it, from using education to restrict rational deliberation of competing conceptions of the good life and the good society."[24] She sees this principle as being compatible with the inculcation of character traits such as "honesty, religious toleration, and mutual respect for persons, that serve as foundations for rational deliberation of different ways of life."[25] Second, Gutmann believes that public education must be founded on the principle of *nondiscrimination*, which provides that "no educable child may be excluded from an education adequate to participating in the political processes that structure choice among good lives."[26]

These philosophical principles may help educators understand the justification for moral education in a democratic society. But of course these principles are not themselves apolitical. They are grounded in a particular vision of the meaning of American democracy and how it might be made to work better, by helping young people acquire the critical moral—as well as the cognitive—tools they need to be more engaged, effective, and responsible citizens. In this sense, there is no getting away from taking some moral-political stand rooted in a vision of America and fighting for it. But at least one can make a reasonable case that, because it focuses on ground rules for facilitating the societywide conversation that constitutes the heart of democracy, this approach at least shows basic respect for all contending belief systems and viewpoints and is committed to making sure that they get a fair hearing. At the same time, it seeks to enhance people's capacities to make sense of what they hear, and ultimately to make moral judgments and act accordingly.

This perspective does not make the tough issues go away. No perspective can, since disagreement and contention are real. All we can do is try to make sure that citizens have the opportunity to have issues presented to them as clearly as possible and that they have the tools with which to think them through.

Some parents will still want creationism to be taught in the public schools, while others will want only evolution by natural selection to be taught. Some citizens will still demand that prayer be allowed in the schools, while others will continue to see school prayer as a violation of the separation of religion and state. Some will argue that curricula that teach about human sexuality and note the fact of diverse sexual orientations promote sexual promiscuity and homosexuality; others will argue that helping students learn about their bodies and sexualities is the best way to keep them healthy and safe, and that acknowledging sexual preference simply promotes the values of tolerance and respect.

These are all real issues, and they have become matters of deep disagreement and contention in what have come to be called America's "culture wars." They will necessarily be fought out in the political and cultural arena, and since young people live, think, and breathe in these arenas, they will necessarily be fought out in schools as well, where young people spend a good deal of their time. It makes sense to give students guidance in dealing with these conflicts, in part by helping them see these conflicts in their historical context so they can make better sense of themselves as responsible historical and moral actors. In this way, we can perhaps move beyond the empty rhetoric, false dichotomies, and general murkiness that have characterized much contemporary debate about education issues. We can, for example, stop denying the profoundly political nature of opposing viewpoints and instead bring political and philosophical differences out into the open, where they can be articulated more clearly and examined more closely. We can also stop posing complex questions in either-or terms, as if they are simple binary opposites. As my portraits of students in the Facing History classroom have shown, it is not really a question of "basics versus values" or "indoctrination versus relativism." Schools need to explore ways to further students' knowledge of traditional content areas as well as to promote their moral growth. Schools can help develop students' capacity for critical moral deliberation and also help them acquire a fixed moral compass for distinguishing right from wrong. Facing History and Ourselves and curricula like it seem to manage these diverse and important tasks very well.

In the long run, by helping students listen to one another attentively and respectfully, and by encouraging them to take well-thought-out moral stands, educational programs that foster critical engagement with social, moral, and political issues may help us at least address, if not resolve, the grave problems we face as a society. We can, we must, hope that through this process students will learn to handle the conflicts they will encounter in the world beyond the classroom more responsibly, and will become the kind of citizens who try to address those conflicts in a democratic spirit. At their best, what these kinds of education programs may offer students is not a blueprint for creating an ideal community that shares a single moral and political outlook. No such community currently exists or is likely to emerge in the future; our society is, for better or worse, simply too heterogeneous, complex, and contentious. Rather, such programs may help young people learn to make better sense of the complex and rapidly changing world they live in, and to develop their own perspective on it as well, in the context of the different social roles they will be called on to play in different contexts. For democracy to work, citizens need to be able to understand and evaluate a broad range of beliefs and ideas, and to act on what they themselves believe. And that is why critical moral education is education for democracy—something we cannot do without.

Notes

Preface

1. Eudora Welty, *The Eye of the Storm: Selected Essays and Reviews* (New York: Vintage Books, 1979), p. 129.

Chapter One

1. At the request of school administrators, the names of the school and its students and teachers have been changed.
2. In the fall of 1989, Boston police responded to a car-phone call from one Charles Stuart, who reported that he and his wife had been shot. When the police located Stuart's car, in the heavily nonwhite Mission Hill neighborhood, they found him bleeding from a gunshot wound; his pregnant wife, Carol DiMaiti Stuart, was already dead by his side, and their prematurely delivered child died in the hospital a short time later. Stuart told police that he and his wife had been robbed and shot by a black man.

    While Charles Stuart recovered from his wound, Boston police aggressively scoured the Mission Hill neighborhood, stopping and frisking numerous young black men as they sought to capture the perpetrator of this heinous crime, as described by Stuart. Eventually police arrested a black man with a criminal record and charged him with Carol Stuart's murder. The case might have ended with this man's conviction and imprisonment, had not Charles Stuart's brother eventually given police information that cast grave doubt on Charles's original version of what had happened in Mission Hill that night. Rather than face the police, Charles Stuart jumped to his death from the Tobin Bridge spanning the Mystic River. It soon became clear that he had murdered his own wife and then wounded himself to cover his crime.

The Carol Stuart murder and the subsequent developments in the case attracted massive local and national media attention. In addition to lending itself to sensationalization, the case raised painful questions about race relations in Boston. It was obvious that, by reporting a black assailant, Charles Stuart had exploited deeply ingrained racial stereotypes and prejudices to cover up his crime. The police apparently shared those attitudes, for they seemed to have accepted Stuart's story without too many questions and responded by launching large-scale search operations on the streets of Mission Hill, operations that suggested little regard for the civil rights of innocent black men. The racial assumptions and attitudes illuminated by the Stuart case were of great concern to many Boston residents.

3. "Shouts Drown Out Rap at Youth Racism Forum," *Boston Globe,* March 27, 1990, p. 21.

4. *Moral Education in the Life of the School,* a report from the ASCD Panel on Moral Education (Alexandria, Va.: Association for Supervision and Curriculum Development, Apr. 1988), pp. 19–20.

5. In fact, the original Facing History and Ourselves *Resource Book* includes a chapter on the Armenian Genocide; other organizational resources, including the 1994 revised *Resource Book,* deal with these "closer-to-home" events more extensively. See, for example, Margot Stern Strom and William S. Parsons, *Facing History and Ourselves: Holocaust and Human Behavior* (Watertown, Mass.: Intentional Educations, Inc., 1982); Alan Stoskopf and Margot Stern Strom, *Choosing to Participate: A Critical Examination of Citizenship in American History* (Brookline, Mass.: Facing History and Ourselves National Foundation, 1990); Fac-

ing History and Ourselves, *Facing History and Ourselves: Resource Book: Holocaust and Human Behavior* (Brookline, Mass.: Facing History and Ourselves National Foundation, 1994).

6. See Melinda Fine, "Collaborative Innovations: Documentation of the Facing History and Ourselves Program at an Essential School," *Teachers College Record*, 1993, 94(4), p. 776.

7. Strom and Parsons, *Facing History and Ourselves: Resource Book: Holocaust and Human Behavior.* It may be useful to note here that the FHAO organization has just completed a substantially revised *Resource Book,* which is structured differently from the text described throughout this study. The new *Resource Book* places much greater emphasis on racism, prejudice, and resistance in the United States, in both contemporary and historical context. See facing History and Ourselves, *Facing History and Ourselves: Resource Book: Holocaust and Human Behavior* (Brookline, Mass.: Facing History and Ourselves National Foundation, 1994).

8. Strom and Parsons, *Facing History and Ourselves: Holocaust and Human Behavior*, p. 14.

Chapter Two

1. For demographic information about the city of Cambridge, see the following resources distributed by the Community Development Department of Cambridge City Hall: *Taking the Pulse of Cambridge: Social and Economic Trends 1980–1990*, pp. 1–2; *Cambridge in Brief; Detailed Race Fact Sheet* (source: U.S. Census 1950–1980); *Comparing Cambridge and Middlesex County; Cambridge Department of Human Service Programs Gateway Cities Grant Application, June 1988, Needs Assessment and Resource Analysis, Description of Newcomer Groups in Cambridge; Language Spoken at Home: Cambridge 1990* (source: U.S. Census of Population and Housing, Summary Tape File 3).

2. *Cambridge School Department Controlled Choice School Assignment Plan* (Cambridge Public School Department, n.d.), p. 9.

3. For information about the Cambridge Public Schools, see the following resources distributed by the Public Information

Office of the Cambridge School Department: *Cambridge School Department Controlled Choice School Assignment Plan; Cambridge Schools at a Glance, 1992–1993; School Choice*—a special report, Carnegie Foundation for the Advancement of Teaching, 1992, pp. 1–42. Information cited is also based on conversations with Bert Giroux, Public Information Director of the Cambridge School Department. Information for national education trends can be found in the National Education Association's *Ranking of the States*, published in 1990.

4. Margot Stern Strom and William S. Parsons, *Facing History and Ourselves: Holocaust and Human Behavior* (Watertown, Mass.: Intentional Educations, Inc., 1982), p. 29.

5. The capitalization in this epigraph is recorded here as it was on the weekly syllabus.

6. *After the First* (Los Angeles: Franciscan Communications Center, 1973). Based on a story by Donald Hall; distributed by Facing History and Ourselves.

7. See Carol Gilligan, *In a Different Voice: Psychological Theory and Women's Development* (Cambridge, Mass.: Harvard University Press, 1982); Carol Gilligan, "Exit-Voice Dilemmas in Adolescent Development," in A. Foxley, M. McPherson, and G. O'Donnell (eds.), *Development, Democracy, and the Art of Trespassing: Essays in Honor of Albert O. Hirschman* (Notre Dame, Ind.: University of Notre Dame Press, 1986); Carol Gilligan, "Adolescent Development Reconsidered," in Charles E. Irwin, Jr. (ed.), *Adolescent Social Behavior and Health*, New Directions for Child Development, no. 37 (San Francisco: Jossey-Bass, 1987); Carol Gilligan, Janie Victoria Ward, and Jill McLean Taylor, with Betty Bardige (eds.), *Mapping the Moral Domain: A Contribution of Women's Thinking to Psychological Theory and Education* (Cambridge, Mass.: Harvard University Press, 1988); Lyn Mikel Brown and Carol Gilligan, *Meeting at the Crossroads: Women's Psychology and Girls' Development* (Cambridge, Mass.: Harvard University Press, 1992).

8. Strom and Parsons, *Facing History and Ourselves: Holocaust and Human Behavior*, p. 38.

Chapter Three

1. Margot Stern Strom and William S. Parsons, *Facing History and Ourselves: Holocaust and Human Behavior* (Watertown, Mass.: Intentional Educations, Inc., 1982), p. 45.
2. Sulamith Ish-Kishor, *The Boy of Old Prague* (New York: Scholastic Book Services, Random House, 1963), pp. 76–77.
3. Ish-Kishor, *The Boy of Old Prague*, p. 90.
4. Strom and Parsons, *Facing History and Ourselves: Holocaust and Human Behavior*, p. 54. Paragraph order reversed.
5. Strom and Parsons, *Facing History and Ourselves: Holocaust and Human Behavior*, p. 14.
6. Strom and Parsons, *Facing History and Ourselves: Holocaust and Human Behavior*, p. 48.

Chapter Four

1. Margot Stern Strom and William S. Parsons, *Facing History and Ourselves: Holocaust and Human Behavior* (Watertown, Mass.: Intentional Educations, Inc., 1982), pp. 383, 387.
2. *Lessons in Hate*, distributed by Intersection Associates, Cambridge, Mass., and available through the FHAO Resource Library, 16 Hurd St., Brookline, Mass. 02146.
3. See Chapter One, note 2.
4. See, for example, Zachary Lockman, "Original Sin," in Zachary Lockman and Joel Beinin (eds.), *Intifada: The Palestinian Uprising Against Israeli Occupation* (Boston: South End Press, 1989), pp. 185–204.
5. *Klan Youth Corps*, distributed by the Anti-Defamation League of B'nai B'rith, New York, and available through the FHAO Resource Library.

Chapter Five

1. See C. D. Kingsley (ed.), *Cardinal Principles of Secondary Education: A Report of the Commission on the Reorganization of Sec-*

ondary Education, Appointed by the National Education Association, bulletin no. 35 (Washington, D.C.: Department of the Interior, Bureau of Education, Government Printing Office, 1918); and National Education Association, *Report of the Committee of Ten on Secondary School Studies* (Washington, D.C.: Government Printing Office, 1893).

2. Harold Rugg, *That Men May Understand* (New York: Doubleday, Doran, and Co., 1941), p. 3.

3. For a discussion of the history of the texts, see Rugg, *That Men May Understand*, pp. 36–52.

4. Rugg, *That Men May Understand*, p. xv.

5. For a fuller discussion of the controversial material included in the texts, see Rugg, *That Men May Understand*, pp. 239–273.

6. Rugg, *That Men May Understand*, pp. 244–245; emphasis in the original.

7. From the *Philadelphia Record*, Feb. 20, 1940; quoted in Rugg, *That Men May Understand*, p. 4.

8. O. K. Armstrong, "Treason in the Textbooks," *American Legion Magazine*, Sept. 1940, p. 8.

9. Peter B. Dow, "Innovation's Perils: An Account of the Origins, Development, Implementation, and Public Reaction to Man: A Course Study," unpublished doctoral dissertation, Graduate School of Education, Harvard University, 1979.

10. For a fuller account of these critiques, see Dow, "Innovation's Perils: An Account of the Origins, Development, Implementation, and Public Reaction to Man: A Course Study."

11. See Max Rafferty, *What They Are Doing To Your Children* (New York: Signet Books, 1966), pp. 56–77.

12. See George Johnson, *Architects of Fear: Conspiracy Theories and Paranoia in American Politics* (Los Angeles: Tarcher, 1983), pp. 163–186.

13. John A. Stormer, *None Dare Call it Treason—25 Years Later* (Florissant, Mo.: Liberty Bell Press, 1990), pp. 153–154.

14. Stormer, *None Dare Call It Treason—25 Years Later*, pp. 153–154.

15. Alan L. Lockwood, "A Critical View of Values Clarification," *Teachers College Record*, Sept. 1975, pp. 35–50.

16. Gordon V. Drake, *Blackboard Power: NEA Threat to America* (Tulsa, Okla.: Christian Crusade Publications, 1968).

17. Chip Berlet and Margaret Quigley, "Traditional Values, Racism, and Christian Theocracy: The Right-Wing Revolt Against the Modern Age," *Public Eye*, Dec. 1992, p. 2.

18. Phyllis Schlafly, "Double Standards in Academic Freedom," *The Phyllis Schlafly Report*, June 1983, p. 1.

19. Onalee McGraw, *Secular Humanism and the Schools: The Issue Whose Time Has Come* (Washington, D.C.: Heritage Foundation, 1976), pp. 4–5.

20. Timothy LaHaye, *The Battle for the Mind* (Old Tappan, N.J.: Revell, 1980).

21. Onalee McGraw, *Secular Humanism and the Schools: The Issue Whose Time Has Come*, p. 12.

22. John Dewey, "What Psychology Can Do for the Teacher," in Reginald Archambault (ed.), *John Dewey on Education: Selected Writings* (New York: Random House, 1964); cited in Lawrence Kohlberg, "The Cognitive-Developmental Approach to Moral Education," in Peter Scharf (ed.), *Readings in Moral Education* (Minneapolis, Minn.: Winston Press, 1978).

23. Onalee McGraw, *Secular Humanism and the Schools: The Issue Whose Time Has Come*, pp. 6–7.

24. Barbara M. Morris, *Change Agents in the Schools: Destroy Your Children, Betray Your Country*, (Upland, Calif.: Barbara M. Morris, 1979), pp. 126–140.

25. See Debra Viadero, "Battle Over Multicultural Education Rises in Intensity: Issue Is What Kind, Not Whether," *Education Week*, Nov. 28, 1990, pp. 1, 11, 13.

26. See "New York's 'Multicultural' Plans Draw Fire from Two Sides" and "Text of Statement by 'Scholars in Defense of History,'" in *Education Week*, Aug. 1, 1990, pp. 33, 38.

27. Samuel Blumenfeld, "Multiculturalism: A Prescription for Moral Anarchy," *Blumenfeld Education Letter*, Sept. 1986, p. 1.

28. In Chip Berlet and Margaret Quigley, "Traditional Values, Racism, and Christian Theocracy: The Right-Wing Revolt Against the Modern Age," p. 6.

29. See Allan Bloom, *The Closing of the American Mind* (New York: Simon & Schuster, 1987), and E. D. Hirsch, Jr., *Cultural Literacy: What Every American Needs to Know* (New York: Vintage Books, 1988).

30. Allan Bloom, *The Closing of the American Mind*, p. 26.

31. Bloom, *The Closing of the American Mind*, pp. 141, 27.

32. Bloom, *The Closing of the American Mind*, p. 39.

33. Bloom, *The Closing of the American Mind*, p. 56.

34. E. D. Hirsch, Jr., *Cultural Literacy: What Every American Needs to Know*, p. xvii.

35. Hirsch, *Cultural Literacy: What Every American Needs to Know*, p. 116.

36. Hirsch, *Cultural Literacy: What Every American Needs to Know*, p. 24.

37. Hirsch, *Cultural Literacy: What Every American Needs to Know*, pp. xii, 12.

38. Hirsch, *Cultural Literacy: What Every American Needs to Know*, p. 18.

39. Hirsch, *Cultural Literacy: What Every American Needs to Know*, p. 133. For a fuller discussion of Hirsch's critique of the Critical Thinking movement and, more generally, of the "romantic formalism" of the past half century (which, he argues, values "form" over "content"), see Hirsch, *Cultural Literacy*, pp. 110–133, where the author addresses "educational democracy" in terms of historical educational debates, most notably *The Committee of Ten Report*, *The Cardinal Principles of Secondary Education*, and the work of John Dewey.

40. Hirsch, *Cultural Literacy: What Every American Needs to Know*, p. 89.

41. Hirsch, *Cultural Literacy: What Every American Needs to Know*, p. 137.

42. Hirsch, *Cultural Literacy: What Every American Needs to Know*, pp. 104, 21.

43. Margot Stern Strom and William S. Parsons, *Facing History and Ourselves: Holocaust and Human Behavior* (Watertown, Mass.: Intentional Educations Inc., 1982), p. 13.

44. Strom and Parsons, *Facing History and Ourselves: Holocaust and Human Behavior*, p. 13.

45. Testimony of Margot Stern Strom to the Subcommittee on Human Resources and Intergovernmental Relations of the Committee on Government Operations, U.S. House of Representatives, Oct. 19, 1988, p. 6.

46. Strom and Parsons, *Facing History and Ourselves: Holocaust and Human Behavior*, p. 7.

47. Strom testimony, p. 13.

48. Strom and Parsons, *Facing History and Ourselves: Holocaust and Human Behavior*, p. 166.

49. Strom and Parsons, *Facing History and Ourselves: Holocaust and Human Behavior*, p. 166. Originally from Haim Ginott, *Teacher and Child* (New York: Macmillan, 1972).

50. Strom testimony, p. 2.

51. Strom testimony, p. 15.

Chapter Six

1. "Child Abuse in the Classroom," *Phyllis Schlafly Report*, Sept. 1984, pp. 2–3.

2. Phyllis Schlafly, *Child Abuse in the Classroom* (Illinois: Pere Marquette Press, 1984).

3. "Child Abuse in the Classroom," *Phyllis Schlafly Report*, Sept. 1984, p. 1.

4. See George Johnson, *Architects of Fear: Conspiracy Theories and Paranoia in American Politics* (Los Angeles: Tarcher, 1983), pp. 163–186.

5. Christopher Hitchens, "Minority Report," *The Nation*, June 8, 1985, p. 694.

6. Hitchens, "Minority Report," p. 694.

7. See Susan Faludi, *Backlash: The Undeclared War Against American Women* (New York: Anchor Books, 1991), p. 263.

8. Schlafly, *Child Abuse in the Classroom*, pp. 435–437.

9. Schlafly, *Child Abuse in the Classroom*, p. 8. Students' comments were published more fully in Lisa Colt, Fanny Connelly, and John Paine, "Facing History and Ourselves: Excerpts from Student Journals," *Moral Education Forum*, summer 1981, and Lisa Colt and Fanny Connelly, "Facing Ourselves: Student Journals," *Independent School*, 1981, 40(3), pp. 17–20.

10. "Forcing Students to Write 'Journals,'" *Phyllis Schlafly Report*, Feb. 1984, p. 3.

11. Schlafly, *Child Abuse in the Classroom*, pp. 14, 24; emphasis in the original.

12. "Highlights from the Testimony of Other Witnesses at the Department of Education Hearings," *Phyllis Schlafly Report*, May 1984, p. 4.

13. Schlafly, *Child Abuse in the Classroom*, p. 12.

14. Schlafly, *Child Abuse in the Classroom*, pp. 435–437.

15. In Chip Berlet and Margaret Quigley, "Traditional Values, Racism, and Christian Theocracy: The Right-Wing Revolt Against the Modern Age," *Public Eye*, Dec. 1992, p. 4.

16. Institute for Cultural Conservatism, Free Congress Research and Education Foundation, *Cultural Conservatism: Toward a New National Agenda* (Lanham, Md.: UPA, Inc., 1987), p.8.

17. "What's Wrong with Global Education?," *Phyllis Schlafly Report*, Apr. 1986, p. 3.

18. Schlafly, *Child Abuse in the Classroom*, p. 436.

19. "Whose Values Do Public Schools Teach?," *Phyllis Schlafly Report*, June 1987, pp. 1–2.

20. Schlafly, *Child Abuse in the Classroom*, p. 437.

21. "Attack on Facing History Fails," *Jewish Advocate*, Oct. 8, 1987.

22. "A History Denied," *L.A. Weekly*, Jan. 6–12, 1989.

23. Schlafly, *Child Abuse in the Classroom*, p. 436.

24. Schlafly, *Child Abuse in the Classroom*, p. 15.

25. "Focus: Colleges Seek to 'Cure' Prejudice," *Education Reporter*, Oct. 1988, p. 3.

26. "Focus: Colleges Seek to 'Cure' Prejudice," p. 3.

27. "Child Abuse in the Classroom," *Phyllis Schlafly Report*, Sept. 1984, p. 1; emphasis in the original.

28. Barbara Morris, *Change Agents in the Schools: Destroy Your Children, Betray Your Country* (Upland, Calif.: Barbara M. Morris, 1979), pp. 70–71.

29. Morris, *Change Agents in the Schools: Destroy Your Children, Betray Your Country*, p. 71.

30. "What's 'Appropriate' for Education Projects?," *Washington Post*, Aug. 4, 1988. Also see Schlafly, *Child Abuse in the Classroom*.

31. "What's 'Appropriate' for Education Projects?"

32. Faludi, *Backlash: The Undeclared War Against American Women*, p. 262.

33. "Holocaust Project Funds: 'Eliminated' by Ideology?," *Washington Post*, Oct. 4, 1988.

34. "Holocaust Project Funds: 'Eliminated' by Ideology?"

35. Letter from Phyllis Schlafly to William Kristol, Aug. 13, 1987; emphasis in the original. Obtained from Facing History and Ourselves.

36. Colt, Connelly, and Paine, "Facing History and Ourselves: Excerpts from Student Journals," p. 34.

37. Colt, Connelly, and Paine, "Facing History and Ourselves: Excerpts from Student Journals," p. 28.

38. Colt and Connelly, "Facing Ourselves: Student Journals," p. 20.

39. "Diffusion Network Backers Criticize Change in Rules," *Education Week*, Aug. 4, 1987, p. 28.

40. "Diffusion Network Backers Criticize Change in Rules," p. 28.

41. "Diffusion Network Backers Criticize Change in Rules," p. 28.

42. Mark Lawrence, "What's 'Appropriate' for Education Projects? Not Department's Review Scheme, Critics Say," *Washington Post*, Aug. 4, 1987.

43. Chester E. Finn, Jr., "Standards for Schools," Letters to the Editor, *Washington Post*, Aug. 1987; response to Aug. 5, 1987 *Washington Post* editorial.

44. See "Unfair to Nazis," *New York Daily News*, Sept. 20, 1987; "Course Faulted for Omitting Nazi Viewpoint," *Boston Globe*, Sept. 21, 1987; "School Program Chided for Lack of Nazi Views," *Courier-Journal*, Sept. 21, 1987.

45. Senator Lowell Weicker in "Senate Votes to End PSP," *Update*, National Dissemination Study Group, Dec. 1987, p. 3.

46. Quoted in the testimony of Margot Stern Strom before the Subcommittee on Human Resources and Intergovernmental Relations of the Committee on Government Operations, U.S. House of Representatives, Oct. 19, 1988, p. 14. "Simon" refers to Sidney Simon, one of the developers of the values clarification approach.

47. Testimony of Max McConkey before the Subcommittee on Human Resources and Intergovernmental Relations of the Committee on Government Operations, U.S. House of Representatives, Oct. 19, 1988, p. 8.

48. "Bias Charged in the Denial of Aid to History Course," *Education Week*, Sept. 14, 1988, p. 18.

49. See "Report Says Emigres with Nazi Ties Form GOP Unit," *Boston Globe*, Sept. 15, 1988, p. 25; "Bush Campaign Committee Contains Figures Linked to Anti-Semitic and Fascist Backgrounds," *Washington Jewish Week*, Sept. 8, 1988, p. 3; "Nazi-Affiliated Emigres and the Republican Party," *Philadelphia Inquirer*, Sept. 18, 1988, p. 4F.

50. Representative Sidney R. Yates, "Inconceivable Thinking on the Part of the Department of Education," *Congressional Record*, Oct. 4, 1988.

51. Statement of Representative Ted Weiss to the Subcommittee on Human Resources and Intergovernmental Relations of the Committee on Government Operations, U.S. House of Representatives, Oct. 19, 1988, p. 1.

52. Statement of Representative Stephen J. Solarz to the Subcommittee on Human Resources and Intergovernmental Relations of the Committee on Government Operations, U.S. House of Representatives, Oct. 19, 1988.

53. Testimony of Shirley Curry to the Subcommittee on Human Resources and Intergovernmental Relations of the Committee on Government Operations, U.S. House of Representatives, Oct. 19, 1988, p. 1.

54. Strom testimony, p. 1.

55. Strom testimony, p. 2.

56. Strom testimony, p. 16.

57. Letter from Lauro F. Cavazos to Congressman Ted Weiss. Obtained from Facing History and Ourselves.

58. "A History Denied," *L.A. Weekly*, Jan. 6–12, 1989, p. 22.

59. "A History Denied," p. 22.

60. Lucy S. Dawidowicz, "How They Teach the Holocaust," *Commentary*, Dec. 1990, p. 25.

61. Dawidowicz, "How They Teach the Holocaust," pp. 25–30.

62. Dawidowicz, "How They Teach the Holocaust," p. 28.

63. "Curriculum Unfair to Nazis," *Together*, Oct. 11, 1987, pp. 1, 19.

64. "Is the Curriculum Biased?," a Statement of the National Association of Scholars, p. 2.

65. Dawidowicz, "How they Teach the Holocaust," p. 25.

66. Dawidowicz, "How They Teach the Holocaust," reprinted in *Network News and Views*, Feb. 1991, pp. 24–31.

67. For an excellent discussion of how the media's framing of an issue affects a local community's understanding of the problem, and how interactions among the media, local community groups, and governmental bodies influence policy outcomes (in this instance regarding the attendance of children infected with the AIDS virus in public schools), see David Kirp, *Learning by Heart: AIDS and Schoolchildren in American Communities* (New Brunswick, N.J.: Rutgers University Press, 1989).

Chapter Seven

1. Rochelle Sharpe, "Efforts to Promote Teaching of Values in Schools Are Sparking Heated Debate Among Lawmakers," *Wall Street Journal*, May 10, 1994, p. A20.

2. See the "Character Education" issue of *Educational Leadership*, Nov. 1993, and Thomas Lickona, *Educating for Character: How Our Schools Can Teach Respect and Responsibility* (New York: Bantam Books), 1991.

3. See E. D. Hirsch, Jr., *Cultural Literacy: What Every American Needs to Know* (New York: Vintage, 1988), pp. 110–133.

4. Sharpe, "Efforts to Promote Teaching of Values in Schools Are Sparking Heated Debate Among Lawmakers." See also the brochure of the Character Education Partnership, available from the organization at 1250 North Pitt St., Alexandria, Va., 22314.

5. See William J. Bennett, "What Value Is Values Education?," *American Educator*, 1980, *4*, 31–32; cited in William Damon, *The Moral Child: Nurturing Children's Natural Moral Growth* (New York: Free Press, 1988), pp. 131–152.

6. Sharpe, "Efforts to Promote Teaching of Values in Schools Are Sparking Heated Debate Among Lawmakers."

7. Former New York City Chancellor of Education Joseph A. Fernandez argued that the media's portrayal of the "Rainbow curriculum" controversy—discussed below—fanned the flames of discord among parents and exacerbated an already tense situation. The media has been, at times, similarly unhelpful in reporting on communities struggling over their public schools' decision to admit students infected with the AIDS virus. See David Kirp, *Learning by Heart: AIDS and Schoolchildren in America's Communities* (New Brunswick, N.J.: Rutgers University Press, 1989).

8. "A Full-Time Volunteer," *New York Times*, May 13, 1993, p. B3.

9. See Kevin Ryan, "Mining the Values in the Curriculum," *Educational Leadership*, Nov. 1993, pp. 16–18.

10. Thomas Lickona, *Educating for Character: How Our Schools Can Teach Respect and Responsibility* (New York: Bantam Books, 1991), p. 7. For a clear and succinct discussion of the evolution of moral education practices in American public schools, see pp. 6–22.

11. William Damon, *The Moral Child: Nurturing Children's Natural Moral Growth* (New York: Free Press, 1990), p. 142. The following discussion of Bennett, Wynne, and Kohlberg is informed more generally by Damon, pp. 141–146.

12. E. A. Wynne, "The Great Tradition in Education: Transmitting Moral Values," *Educational Leadership*, 1986, *43*, pp. 4–9; quoted in Damon, *The Moral Child: Nurturing Children's Natural Moral Growth*, p. 142.

13. "Focus: Colleges Seek to 'Cure' Prejudice," *Education Reporter*, Oct. 1988, p. 3.

14. W. J. Bennett and E. J. Delattre, "A Moral Education: Some Thoughts on How Best to Achieve It," *American Educator*, 1978, *3*, 6–9; quoted in Damon, *The Moral Child*, p. 144.

15. Phyllis Schlafly, *Child Abuse in the Classroom* (Illinois: Pere Marquette Press, 1980), pp. 14, 24; emphasis in the original.

16. My discussion of the various elements that make up this "middle ground" is indebted to William Damon, *The Moral Child: Nurturing Children's Natural Moral Growth*, pp. 149–152.

17. Larry Rohter, "Battle Over Patriotism Curriculum," *New York Times*, May 15, 1994, p. 22.

18. Peter West, "Florida Union Vows to Fight District's 'Americanism' Policy," *Education Week*, May 25, 1994, p. 3.

19. "Board Sets a Vote on Policy to Teach That U.S. Is Superior," *New York Times*, June 23, 1994.

20. West, "Florida Union Vows to Fight District's 'Americanism' Policy," p. 3.

21. See People for the American Way, *Attacks on the Freedom to Learn: 1992–1993 Report* (Washington, D.C.: People for the American Way, 1993).

22. Rohter, "Battle Over Patriotism Curriculum," p. 22.

23. Amy Gutmann, *Democratic Education* (Princeton, N.J.: Princeton University Press, 1987), p. 39.

24. Gutmann, *Democratic Education*, p. 44.

25. Gutmann, *Democratic Education*, p. 44.

26. Gutmann, *Democratic Education*, p. 45.

Index

211

The Author

MELINDA FINE received her B.A. degree (1981) from Dartmouth College with a specal honors major in feminist theory, literature, and social change, and her Ed.M. (1988) and Ed.D. (1991) degrees from Harvard University. She is an educational research and program development consultant whose clients include youth development organizations, curriculum development groups, school reform initiatives, and public television. From 1984 to 1986, she served as the international coordinator of the National Nuclear Weapons Freeze Campaign. From 1991 to 1993, she served as the assistant director of research for the Children Television Workshop's *Ghostwriter* television series. She has worked with the Facing History and Ourselves organization since 1989 as an independent research consultant and a member of the organization's national teacher training team. Her research interests include moral development and social responsibility, school reform, critical thinking, educational equity and development for girls, conflict resolution, and urban education.

Fine's publications include "You Can't Just Say That the Only Ones Who Can Speak Are Those Who Agree with Your Position: Political Discourse in the Classroom" (*Harvard Educational Review*, 1993, 63[4], 412–433), "Collaborative Innovations: Documentation of the Facing History and Ourselves Program at an Essential School" (*Teachers College Record*, 1993, 94[4], 771–789), and "Facing History and Ourselves: Portrait of a Classroom" (*Educational Leadership* [Dec. 1991/Jan. 1992, pp. 44–49]), for which she received the 1992 Edpress feature article award.